"THIS BOOK IS DEDICATED TO THE AGE OF AI THAT UNEQUIVOCALLY SURPRISED THE WORLD IN 2023 AND THE UTILIZATION OF THIS TECHNOLOGY FOR INNOVATORS TO THRIVE IN A NEW ERA."

- K.A. Betancourt

DREAMING IN DIGITAL
THE AGE OF AI CINEMA

FIRST EDITION, 2026
DREAMING IN DIGITAL SERIES, VOLUME IV
PUBLISHED BY COSMIC LION BOOK CLUB PUBLISHING
AN INDEPENDENT IMPRINT

ISBN: 979-8-9945160-0-3 (PAPERBACK)
ISBN: 979-8-9945160-1-0 (HARDCOVER)

DREAMING IN DIGITAL

THE AGE OF AI CINEMA

By K.A.Betancourt

COSMIC LION BOOK CLUB PUBLISHING

. . . a love letter for ai film

You feel it too — in the culture, in the technology. The world of entertainment is shifting, and it's happening fast. Movie theaters are still trying to find their place in a world reshaped by streaming and shifting audience habits, while blockbusters arrive on streaming platforms within weeks. Productions move overseas, projects are shelved midstream, and the system that once defined Hollywood feels increasingly fragile. For nearly a century, cinema operated on prestige, control, and gatekeeping. Directors were elevated to icons, access was limited, and creative power was concentrated in the hands of a few. That model is cracking—*rapidly*.

This isn't the first time cinema has changed. There was a period when working with physical film was so expensive and complex that only a small group could create—and even fewer could distribute. The digital revolution widened that door, and as cameras became smaller, cheaper, and more powerful, the barriers continued to fall. By the time smartphones entered the conversation, the idea that cinematic tools belonged only to studios was already fading; award-winning directors were shooting entire films on devices that fit in a pocket. Artificial intelligence marks the next phase of this progression. It accelerates experimentation and visual exploration at a scale that was previously unreachable.

Suddenly, everything is possible—and that can feel overwhelming. The expanding landscape of AI tools and workflows makes it difficult to know where to begin or how to choose the right approach. A simple search for "AI video" or "text-to-image generation" reveals dozens of platforms promising similar results—each with different models, interfaces, and trade-offs. Deciding which tools truly support creative intent has become its own challenge. This is where this book comes in.

This book, The Age of AI Cinema, focuses on which tools will help you develop your cinema in the most efficient way, along with the craftsmanship and skills that make creative work intentional and memorable. From text prompting and narrative structure to camera language, sound design, visual formulas, and character consistency, these elements form a framework for building cohesive worlds and assembling complete cinematic experiences with clarity, using AI.

At its core, this work isn't about replacing creativity—it's about redefining it. When the fundamentals are understood deeply enough, tools fall away, leaving space for your voice, your perspective, and the stories only you can tell. Cinema will be shaped by individuals around the world who understand emotion, culture, and visual language. It won't be defined by budgets or permission, but by clarity of vision and the confidence to express it. *This is your moment to create.* **Let's go!**

TABLE OF CONTENTS

GETTING STARTED

Getting Started

Since AI tools first emerged, they've evolved at a pace that's been difficult to keep up with. Early on, much of the conversation lived at the edge of what was newly possible. Over time, however, the technology began to settle. As tools move into longer adoption cycles, the focus has shifted away from what's new this week and toward what's reliable and creatively meaningful. This book was written from within that transition—at the point where a new way of creating cinema begins to take shape with clarity and intention.

With that in mind, this book isn't meant to be rushed through. Each chapter is designed to stand on its own, allowing you to move between concepts as your projects evolve. While tools will continue to change, the creative fundamentals remain consistent. Think of this book as a modular guide—return to sections as needed, apply what resonates, and build your workflow in a way that supports your own creative process. There is no single correct way to create with AI. Experimentation is part of the process, and your judgment matters. The goal isn't perfection—it's clarity. As you work through these ideas, trust your instincts, stay curious, and allow your creative voice to lead. This book is here to support that journey, helping you shape stories, worlds, and cinematic experiences on your own terms.

AI Tools $ubscriptions

AI tools do come with real costs, most often in the form of subscriptions or credit-based pricing. Depending on the platform, monthly plans can range from smaller starter tiers around $10–$15 to more advanced options that reach $100 per month or more, with many tools also offering annual plans. The most important consideration at this stage is awareness—keeping track of what you sign up for, using tools with intention, and canceling them when they're no longer serving your work.

For the purposes of this book, some of the image and video creation examples are built using Midjourney, which offers entry-level plans starting at $10 per month. Midjourney is used as a practical working example because of its consistency and growth over the years—not as a sponsorship or endorsement. I'm not affiliated with the platform or any other company mentioned in this book. Different tools will appear throughout as they become relevant, showing how various stages of your process connect and where they're most useful. The focus is on how tools support creative decisions based on your project's needs. The goal is to move ideas from early tests into completed cinematic work, not to maintain a long list of subscriptions.

NAVIGATING MIDJOURNEY

Getting Started with Midjourney

Midjourney is a generative artificial intelligence program developed by the independent research lab Midjourney, Inc., based in San Francisco, and is widely regarded for its high-quality image generation using natural language text prompts. The platform has evolved through multiple major updates and is currently operating on Version 7, with Version 8 on the horizon. Each release has focused on improving image quality, coherence, and visual consistency across subjects and environments. Midjourney has also introduced video generation, an exciting expansion that marked a meaningful shift beyond static imagery and opened new possibilities for motion-based visual storytelling.

Where to Access Midjourney

→ www.midjourney.com

Previously, Midjourney was accessible only through a Discord server. My earlier books walked through that setup step by step; however, for this updated book, we will be working solely within the web-based experience of Midjourney. If you're interested in setting up the Discord server, there are tutorials available online, or you can reference my previous books.

To follow along with the examples in this section, you'll need an active Midjourney subscription, as mentioned earlier. If you're not ready to subscribe just yet, feel free to read through the book and return to the hands-on examples when you are.

Why Midjourney?

Because without captivating art, there is no captivating AI cinema.

After testing a wide range of AI image generators, Midjourney has consistently stood out for its visual quality, compositional control, and reliability. While many tools can generate images, fewer produce results that feel intentional, cinematic, and visually cohesive. When the goal is to create work with emotional weight or cinematic presence, the underlying imagery matters. In visual storytelling, a film is only as strong as its art, and in AI cinema, that foundation begins with the image.

Midjourney excels at translating structured text prompts into images with depth, atmosphere, and visual clarity. It rewards thoughtful prompting and offers a level of control that supports cinematic thinking rather than working against it. For that reason, this book uses Midjourney as the primary image-generation tool—not because it is the only option, but because it provides a strong and consistent foundation for building high-quality visual work. We'll begin with the fundamentals of image creation before expanding into more advanced concepts later in the book.

Copyright and Ownership When Using Midjourney

Midjourney's Terms of Service grant you ownership of the images and videos you generate with its service, including the right to use them commercially in your creative work, such as film festival submissions, proof-of-concept reels, branded content, and other projects — even if you cancel your subscription later, provided the work was created while you were a paid member. There are a few important conditions to be aware of: if you upscaled or incorporated an image originally created by another user, that asset remains owned by the original creator and you need their permission to use it. Additionally, if you are using the service on behalf of a business with more than $1,000,000 USD in annual revenue, Midjourney requires a Pro or Mega plan for commercial use rights. Copyright law around AI-generated work is still evolving, and definitions of ownership and rights can vary by jurisdiction. For that reason, it's important to review Midjourney's Terms of Service periodically to ensure your use continues to align with the latest guidelines.

AI Ethics in Cinema

When working with AI in filmmaking, transparency matters. Whether you're submitting to a film festival, pitching a proof of concept, or releasing branded content, it's important to be clear about how AI played a role in your process. Audiences, collaborators, and clients deserve honesty, and transparency helps establish trust so the work can be understood on its own terms.

Ethical considerations, however, go beyond disclosure. Many AI systems were trained on large datasets that include existing artworks, sometimes without the knowledge or consent of the original creators. As a result, some outputs can feel less like inspiration and more like direct replication. This tension has sparked ongoing debate and highlights how close the line can be between drawing influence and appropriating style.

In practice, this means working with intention. Be open about how AI is used, avoid over-reliance on another artist's recognizable style or copyrighted characters, and aim for transformation rather than imitation. Treat prompts and references as starting points, not shortcuts, and focus on developing a voice that feels distinctly your own.

AI isn't here to replace artists — it's a tool that can expand what's possible when used thoughtfully. Work that feels original and grounded in personal vision tends to resonate more deeply, while work that leans too heavily on replication often feels hollow. This book can't dictate how you use these tools, but it can surface the questions worth considering, so you're equipped to create with awareness, responsibility, and confidence as the AI landscape continues to evolve.

Overview of Midjourney Tools

1. **Image Generation from Text Prompts**
   Translate structured natural text into high-quality, expressive images.

2. **AI Videos from Images**
   Translate still images into motion sequences with options to extend clips.

3. **Edit Images**
   Edit generated AI images by erasing and regenerating specific areas, as well as adjusting framing through resizing, aspect ratio, and zooming to refine composition.

4. **Style Consistency**
   Carry a visual language across multiple images using references and style codes.

5. **Character Consistency**
   Create consistent characters across scenes while maintaining recognizable features, proportions, and overall identity.

6. **Reference Images**
   Guide composition, and visual direction by incorporating reference images.

7. **Apply Personalization Profiles / Moodboards**
   Personalized machine learning that shapes outputs to better reflect your aesthetic preferences over time.

8. **Parameters**
   Dial in style, character, and image references, variation, and emphasis through parameter codes.

9. **Upload an Image and Generate the Text Prompt**
   Utilize the "Describe" feature for an uploaded image and have Midjourney provide the text prompts.

10. **Explore New Prompts Daily**
    Browse the Explore page for a live stream of generated images and prompts, or use the search bar to find examples, styles, and visual directions for inspiration and learning.

Explore Page

As a beginner—*and even more so as an expert*—this will quickly become one of your favorite places to spend time on Midjourney. The **Explore page** offers nearly endless inspiration, paired with real text prompts that show AI video and image examples. It's an easy way to spark ideas, run prompts, and observe how different words, structures, and styles influence the final result.

Within the Explore page, you'll see several tabs, including Videos, Images, and Styles. The Styles tab is especially worth spending time with from an artistic perspective, which is why this book includes a dedicated chapter focused entirely on style exploration and development.

Copying a Prompt from the Explore Page

Hover over an image and click the [T] icon to view and copy the text prompt used to create it.*Tip: Instead of generating every image you like, save it using the heart icon. This adds the image and its prompt to your "Likes" tab, making it easy to return to your favorite references later without cluttering your workspace or wasting credits if you don't need it for a project.

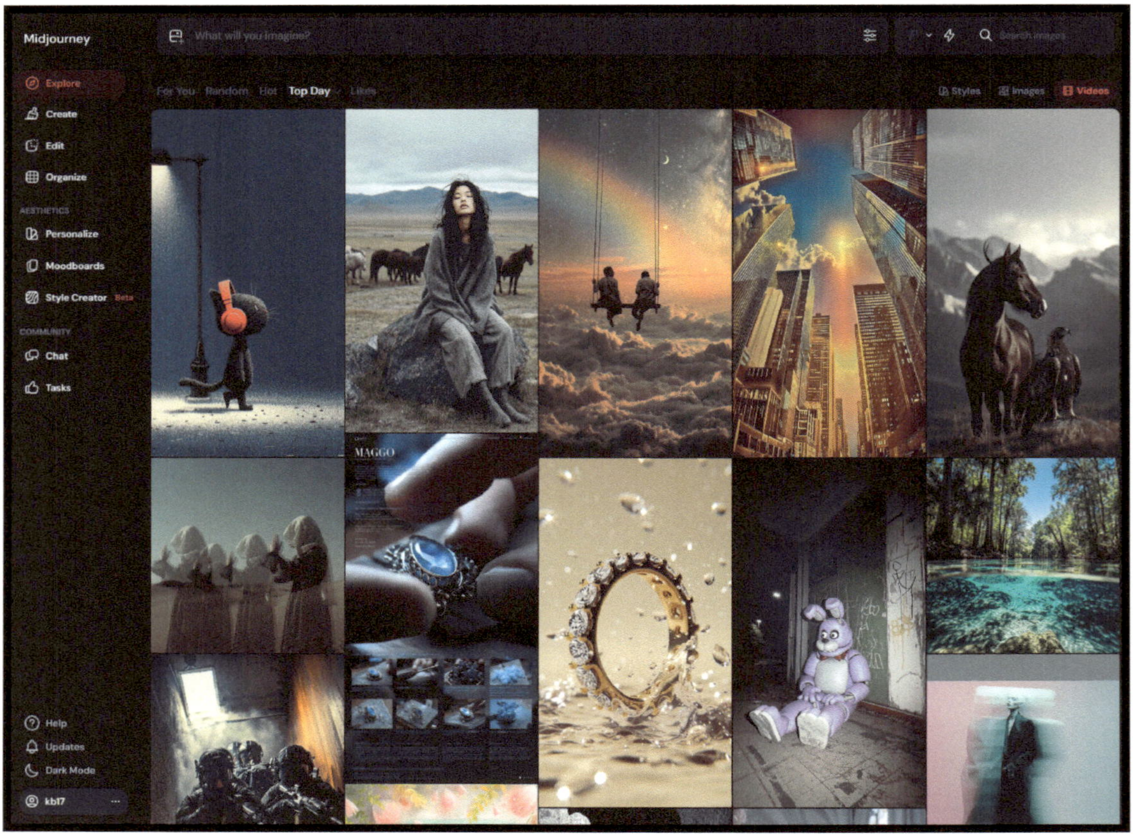

Screenshot as of January 2026

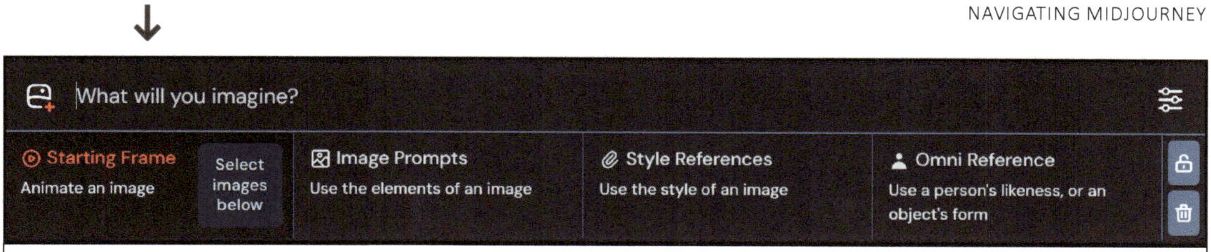

What will you imagine?

This area of Midjourney is the central workspace where all image and video creation begins. It's where language, references, and controls come together to shape what the system generates. Rather than thinking of this space as a single input field, it helps to understand it as a flexible composition area—one that supports text, images, style guidance, and motion.

At its core, this is where you enter your text prompt. The prompt communicates the subject, environment, mood, and intent behind what you want to create. Around this input, Midjourney provides tools that allow you to guide the system visually rather than relying on text alone.

Image Prompts (References)

You can upload images directly into this space to act as visual references. These images can influence composition, subject matter, framing, or overall direction. Image references are especially useful when you want to anchor a prompt to a specific visual idea rather than starting from text alone.

Style References

Style references allow you to guide the aesthetic language of an image using an existing visual. Instead of describing a look entirely in words, you can reference an image whose lighting, color, texture, or artistic treatment you want to carry forward. Because style plays such a significant role in cinematic work, there is a dedicated chapter later in this book focused entirely on developing and controlling style.

Omni Reference

Omni Reference is used for character references that help maintain visual consistency when working with people, creatures, or recognizable forms across multiple scenes—especially important for AI cinema. By referencing an existing character image, you can preserve identity, proportions, and key features from scene to scene. Character consistency is especially important for narrative and cinematic projects and is covered in more depth in a later chapter.

Sliders and Controls

In addition to text and images, this area includes sliders and controls that adjust how the system interprets your prompt. These settings influence elements such as stylization, variation, framing, and format. While these controls can be adjusted visually, Midjourney translates them into parameters behind the scenes. This book will explain how to read and understand those parameters so you remain in control, whether you use sliders or text.

Video, Starting Frames, and Ending Frames

When working with video, this same space allows you to define starting frames, ending frames, low/high motion and looping video. In the AI Video section, we'll explore when and why these options are effective—and when they are not. Here, images act as the foundation for movement, with motion generated from a single frame. Video workflows will be explored further once other important fundamentals are established.

Describe

When you upload an image into this area and click and drag, Midjourney presents a Describe box that allows you to drag the image into a dedicated box. This feature analyzes the visual and generates a text-based prompt describing its key elements, structure, and style. It's a useful way to understand how Midjourney interprets an image, and it can serve as a strong starting point for remixing, refining, or rebuilding a prompt using your own language and intent.

Viewing and Managing Your Generated Images

Create | The Create tab is where generation happens in real time. This is the active workspace where you enter text prompts, adjust settings, and generate new images or video outputs. It's designed for working in clustered sequences—allowing you to rerun prompts, explore variations, and refine ideas as they take shape.

Organize | The Organize tab functions as your visual archive. This is where completed generations appear after they're created, allowing you to review past work, compare results, and group images into folders. For longer projects or cinematic workflows, the Organize tab helps maintain clarity by keeping visuals accessible within a grid-based layout. You can also search the Organize tab by using keywords to quickly locate images you've previously generated.

TEXT PROMPTING

What is a Text Prompt?

A text prompt is the language bridge between your imagination and an AI-generated image or video, translating an idea from your mind into something visual, structured, and interpretable by an AI system. More than a simple description, a strong text prompt establishes perspective, defines priority, and communicates intent. It guides the system toward what matters most—what should be seen first, what sets the mood, and how the final image should feel. When written with clarity, a text prompt becomes less about listing details and more about directing vision, which we will break down next.

Order of Importance in a Text Prompt

When writing a text prompt, think in terms of visual weight and decision hierarchy. A strong prompt moves from the most influential choices to the least, allowing the AI to resolve structure before style and parameters. Begin with perspective to establish where the camera is positioned, then identify the main subject so the image has a clear focal point. From there, add descriptive details and environment to build mood and context, while style and parameters refine the final look. When prompts follow this order, the AI is less likely to guess, overcompensate, or produce generic results—and more likely to generate images that clearly reflect your original idea.

If you'd like to follow along with the text prompt example, head to Midjourney. You'll need a basic subscription plan to generate images, and you'll enter the prompt in the "What will you imagine?" field. The example prompt is color-coded to reflect the order of importance.

Perspective → Main Subject → Environment → Descriptive Details → Style → Parameters

Text Prompt Example

eye-level view, woman seated alone at a small café table, French Quarter New Orleans, wrought iron balcony shadows falling across the sidewalk, vintage café chairs, quiet morning light, she holds a ceramic coffee cup mid-pause, relaxed posture, thoughtful expression, linen blouse, soft neutral tones, warm skin, subtle motion in the air, historic textures, peeling pastel walls, shuttered windows, hand-drawn illustrative style, painterly lines, editorial illustration, cinematic softness, restrained color palette, calm, intimate, timeless --ar 9:16 --v 7

Breaking Down Text Prompting

Now that you've seen a balanced text prompt, we will look more closely at how it's structured. Each part of the prompt plays a distinct role, and understanding how these elements work together allows you to write with greater clarity and control.

Perspective

In simple terms, perspective answers *"Where is the camera?"*

Perspective defines how the scene is viewed by establishing where the viewer is positioned and how the image is framed. Beginning with perspective helps set the overall composition before any subjects or details are introduced. We will explore how to prompt for different cameras, camera angles, and shot composition types more thoroughly in the Cameras and Angles chapter later in this book. **Examples: eye-level view, overhead view, wide shot, close-up, bird's-eye view, etc.**

Main Subject

In simple terms, the main subject answers *"What am I looking at?"*

The main subject is what the image is about and should be the clearest, most important element in the prompt. A strong prompt usually focuses on one clear subject rather than several competing ones. **Examples: man painting a mural, modern beach house, giraffe eating from a tree.**

Environment

In simple terms, the environment answers *"Where is this happening?"*

Environment describes where the subject exists. This anchors the image in a specific place or context and helps the system understand architectural, cultural, or atmospheric cues. Placing environment early helps prevent the system from defaulting to generic settings. **Examples: French Quarter New Orleans, desert landscape, quiet suburban street, coastal village.**

Descriptive Details

In simple terms, the descriptive details answer *"What does it look and feel like?"*

Descriptive details add texture, mood, and nuance. These are the words that help the image feel specific and alive without overpowering the subject. These details should support the subject and environment, not compete with them. **Examples: quiet morning light, relaxed posture, soft neutral tones, peeling pastel wallpaper.**

Style

In simple terms, style answers *"How should this be rendered artistically?"*

Style defines the visual language of the image. This is where you guide the system toward illustration, realism, cinematic lighting, 3D animation, or a specific artistic look. Style works best after the scene itself has been clearly established in the prompt. **Examples: hand-drawn, cinematic realism, 3D, 2D, watercolor, paint strokes, illustrative.**

Parameters

Parameters are technical instructions that control how the system interprets and finalizes your prompt. While descriptive words define what you want to see, parameters determine how the system behaves during generation. Placed at the end of a prompt, they operate behind the scenes—locking in elements such as aspect ratio, model behavior, and output constraints. In cinematic workflows, parameters enable repeatability, visual continuity, and the ability to scale ideas into sequences rather than one-off images.

Parameters can be applied either by writing them directly into the prompt or by adjusting sliders in the dropdown menu where you enter your text. When sliders are used, Midjourney automatically converts those settings into parameter codes if the prompt is copied and pasted. Understanding what these codes represent helps remove confusion and allows you to work with greater confidence and control over your results.

Key Parameter Codes

--ar (Aspect Ratio)
Controls the shape and framing of the image (for example, square, vertical, horizontal).
Example: --ar 9:16 for vertical or --ar 16:9 for cinematic widescreen.

--v (Version of Midjourney)
The version parameter determines which underlying Midjourney model is used to generate the image. Newer versions typically offer improved realism, coherence, and understanding of prompts, while older versions may behave differently or produce more stylized results. If no version is specified, Midjourney will default to the most recent available model at the time of generation. **Example:** --v 7

--weird (Weirdness)
With a range of 0–3000, higher values push results toward unexpected compositions and less polished aesthetics. In simple terms, it answers, *"How strange can this be?"* **Example:** --weird 500

--stylize (Stylization)
Stylize controls how strongly Midjourney applies its artistic interpretation to your prompt. With a range of 0–1000, higher values increase the intensity of the style without changing the style itself.
Example: --s 550

--chaos (also known as Variety)
Chaos controls how much variation the system introduces when interpreting your prompt. With a range of 0–100, higher values allow for a wider range of interpretations, while lower values produce more consistent, predictable results. In simple terms, it answers, *"How much variation do I want?"*

Using ChatGPT to Help Write Your Text Prompts

Understanding the structure of text prompts is essential for achieving consistent, reliable results. AI tools perform best when guided by clear structure and intentional decisions. Once this foundation is in place, tools like OpenAI's ChatGPT can be used to generate prompts more efficiently. Instead of starting from scratch for each cinematic project or character scene, you can establish a clear precedent with ChatGPT in the following ways.

1. Establish the collaboration.

Tell ChatGPT that you will be building Midjourney text prompts together, and that prompts should be structured and ready to paste directly into Midjourney.

2. Set your foundation.

Ask ChatGPT to remember the order of importance outlined earlier in this book, along with your preferences for camera type, lighting, style, aspect ratio, and overall visual tone. These elements will be expanded on throughout the book, but setting them early helps create consistency.

3. Build and continue scenes.

Once your signature look and character design are established, continue prompting naturally. **For example:** *"Let's create a Midjourney prompt for this scene, keeping the same style and camera, but now the character has entered the room."* ChatGPT can then generate new prompts that build on what's already been defined.

A Few Things to Keep in Mind

- Start simple, then refine. Begin with the core idea and add only what serves the image. Avoid stacking too many concepts at once—if results feel inconsistent, ideas may be competing.
- Treat prompts as drafts. Small word changes can produce meaningful shifts in results.
- Consistency comes from repetition, not perfection. Reusing structure and preferences builds a recognizable visual language over time with ChatGPT.
- Trust your eye over the output. If an image technically works but doesn't feel right, adjust the prompt. You can also share the image with ChatGPT to help refine the wording or structure your text prompt more effectively.

Before moving on, it's important to remember that AI-assisted prompting does not replace your creative role. Tools like ChatGPT don't see images, sense tone, or exercise taste—its strength lies in organizing language, maintaining structure, and supporting continuity. Expect to refine phrasing, remove excess detail, and shift emphasis as your intent clarifies. Used intentionally, AI saves time by handling early structure, allowing you to focus on refinement, authorship, and final creative decisions in your AI cinema.

ASPECT RATIO + PIXELS

Aspect Ratio: What It Means and Why It Matters

If you're new to this space, aspect ratio may not feel intuitive at first—so let's take a moment to break it down. Aspect ratio doesn't define the quality of an image; it defines the shape of the frame. It describes the proportional relationship between an image's width and height, expressed as formats like 16:9, 9:16, or 1:1.

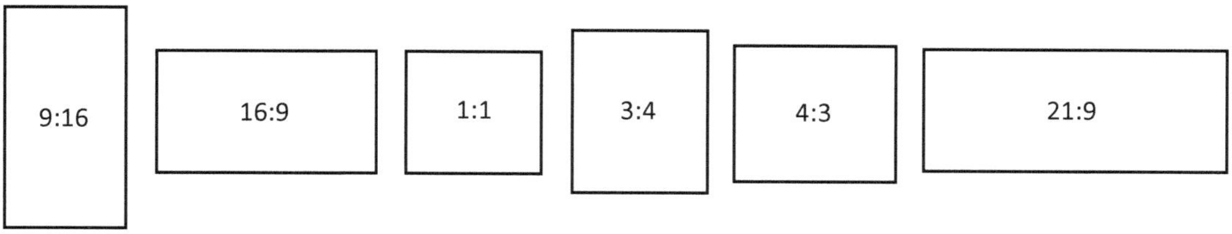

In Midjourney text prompting, the aspect ratio is controlled using the **--ar** parameter and must be placed at the end of a text-to-image prompt, or it will be flagged as an error. **If no aspect ratio is specified, Midjourney defaults to a square format (1:1).**

Think of it this way: aspect ratio determines how your story is framed, not how sharp or detailed it appears. A **16:9** ratio creates a widescreen, cinematic feel commonly used in film and on YouTube. A **9:16** ratio flips the frame vertically, making it ideal for TikTok, Instagram Reels, and mobile storytelling. A **1:1** ratio keeps the composition square and centered, which works well for product imagery. Aspect ratio choices should be made early, especially when building toward AI cinema, as they influence composition decisions throughout your project. In AI image generation, choosing the right aspect ratio shapes how a viewer experiences a moment. It defines mood, composition, and focus—whether you're framing an intimate portrait or revealing the full scope of a cinematic world.

Understanding Pixels and Image Quality

While aspect ratio determines shape, pixels determine clarity. Every digital image is made up of thousands—or often millions—of tiny colored squares called pixels, and the more pixels an image contains, the sharper and more detailed it appears. This is commonly referred to as resolution, written as values like 1920×1080 (HD), 3840×2160 (4K), or 7680×4320 (8K). The first number represents width in pixels, and the second represents height. Increasing resolution does not change framing or aspect ratio as long as both dimensions scale proportionally—only uneven changes alter the aspect ratio. So you can have an image that is 1920×1080 or 7680×4320, and both will still have the same 16:9 aspect ratio.

Think of pixels as the building blocks of your image: the more pixels, the clearer the image is, with richer textures and a more professional result. While you can't directly set pixel count in Midjourney, it does offer upscaling options after an image is generated, allowing you to increase resolution without changing the original framing. Additional upscaling can also be done using external tools if needed. For professional work, HD (1920×1080, a 16:9 ratio) is a reliable baseline, while 4K (3840×2160) offers greater flexibility for editing, large displays, and high-end delivery. In AI cinema, resolution is always a balance—higher pixel counts add realism and depth, but extremely high resolutions can slow workflows and computer processing time. Let your project guide your choices.

CAMERAS & ANGLES

Directing the Shot: Cameras, Angles, and Visual Storytelling in AI Cinema

Camera types and camera angles are two of the most powerful tools in cinema, and the same is true in AI image generation. The moment you start telling the model **HOW** to see—not just what to see—your images transform from simple visuals into intentional, cinematic compositions. In this section, we'll break down both camera types and camera angles, and more importantly, the key words you can use in your text prompts to enhance your visual storytelling. You'll see how adding certain terms can shape mood, story, and realism in text-to-image prompting. Once you understand how to "place the camera," your perspective when prompting AI scenes will instantly feel more professional, immersive, and emotionally grounded.

Types of Cameras in Text-to-Image Prompting for AI Cinema

One of the most powerful aspects of AI cinema and text prompting is the ability to change camera style instantly and seamlessly to match your aesthetic goals. A simple shift in camera type can dramatically transform the look, mood, and professionalism of an image—yet many creators overlook how significant this impact can be. In this section, we'll focus on camera types as they function within Midjourney, which currently offers a strong range of cinematic styles and flexible interpretation. Understanding how these camera cues are read by the system gives you greater control over tone, realism, and visual intent.

Over the next few pages, you'll see several camera-type examples you can add directly to your text prompts to elevate your visuals from amateur to cinematic-quality results. Example prompts are included, with specific camera keywords highlighted, since these terms carry weight in text prompting and help the system understand the visual style you're aiming to achieve. Some of these differences may feel subtle—or you may even wonder if anything changed at all. In many cases, that's exactly how camera styles work, both in AI and in real cinema: their influence is often quiet, shaping tone, depth, and emotional texture rather than producing dramatic, obvious shifts.

As you continue experimenting, you'll begin to notice how different camera types affect sharpness, color behavior, depth of field, and the overall mood of a scene. With that foundation in mind, here's a quick reference list of camera-type keywords you can use in your own prompts. These terms help guide the AI toward a specific visual language, making it easier to maintain consistency and intention across future scenes.

Camera Keywords

Hasselblad X2D 100C
Leica M11
IMAX camera
Nikon D850
Canon EOS R5
Sony A7R IV
RED Komodo

ARRI Alexa 35
GoPro Hero perspective
iPhone cinematic camera
DSLR photography style
Medium format camera
Ultra-wide lens
Telephoto lens

Macro lens
Tilt-shift lens
Fisheye lens
Vintage film camera
Point-and-shoot camera look
Drone photography style

Handheld documentary camera
Cinematic studio camera
Portrait lens 85mm
35mm street photography lens
24mm wide-angle lens
First-person POV camera

Film Look & Aesthetic Keywords

Kodak Portra 400
Kodak Vision3 250D
Kodak Vision3 500T
Fujifilm Pro 400H
Ilford HP5 black-and-white
35mm film look
70mm film look

Cool daylight film tone
Retro 1970s film aesthetic
1990s analog aesthetic
Muted cinematic color grade
High-contrast film grade
Soft bloom highlights
Vintage 80's

Soft film grain
Heavy film grain
Halation glow
Chromatic aberration
Vintage film fade
Warm tungsten film tone
Polaroid

CineStill 800T look
Washed-film palette
Overexposed film style
Underexposed analog look
Dust and scratch texture
Old lens vignette
Film burn / light leak

Camera Type Examples

Camera Keyword: Nikon F2 vintage film camera

Film Look Keyword: Kodak 35mm film

Midjourney Prompt: cinematic portrait of a young Black man with a soft blonde afro and striking green eyes, wearing large retro over-ear headphones, sitting on a vintage 1970s couch in a detailed basement. He is looking down at an open book resting in his hands as he reads, calm, focused expression. wood-paneled walls, record player, stacks of vinyls, warm tungsten lamps, retro patterned rug, scattered magazines, analog 1970s clutter. shot on **Kodak 35mm film,** captured with a **Nikon F2 vintage film camera**, authentic 1970s color cast, soft film grain, warm tones, halation around lights. cozy cinematic mood, shallow depth of field with gentle film softness, highly detailed environment --ar 16:9

Camera Keyword: Leica M11 digital rangefinder

Film Look Keyword: intimate documentary style

Midjourney Prompt: cinematic portrait of a young Black man with a soft blonde afro and striking green eyes, wearing large retro over-ear headphones, sitting on a vintage 1970s couch in a detailed basement. He is looking down at an open book resting in his hands, calm introspective expression. wood-paneled walls, record player, stacks of vinyls, warm tungsten lamps, retro patterned rug, scattered magazines, natural basement details. captured with a **Leica M11 digital rangefinder camera,** signature Leica micro-contrast, soft natural tonal rolloff, intimate documentary style, clean highlights, warm realistic skin tones, shallow depth of field with gentle falloff, subtle cinematic grain --ar 16:9 --raw

Camera Keyword: Hasselblad X2D 100C
Film Look Keyword: HD Digital Cinematic

Midjourney Prompt: cinematic portrait of a young Black man with a soft blonde afro and striking green eyes, wearing large retro over-ear headphones, sitting on a vintage 1970s couch in a detailed basement. He is looking down at an open book resting in his hands as he reads, calm focused expression. wood-paneled walls, record player, stacks of vinyls, warm tungsten lamps, retro patterned rug, scattered magazines, rich 1970s basement details. captured with a Hasselblad X2D 100C digital camera, crisp HD clarity, clean modern sharpness, soft diffused lighting, realistic skin tones, gentle depth of field, cinematic realism, highly detailed environment --ar 16:9 --raw

Standard vs Raw (--raw) Rendering

By default, Midjourney applies its standard rendering, which adds a layer of stylistic polish to your prompt. When the **--raw** parameter is used, this built-in styling is reduced, causing the system to follow your wording more literally. Raw mode is useful when precision matters more than polish, such as in cinematic realism or product-focused imagery.

Camera Keyword: IMAX 65mm large-format camera

Film Look Keyword: epic scale, atmospheric, panoramic, cinematic, realism

Midjourney Prompt: epic cinematic wide shot of a young Black man with a soft blonde afro and striking green eyes standing alone on a dramatic coastal cliff at sunrise, wind blowing gently through his hair. He wears a long textured coat, slightly open, revealing a simple shirt underneath. The ocean crashes far below, golden sunlight cutting through low fog, creating sweeping atmospheric layers. towering cliffs extend into the horizon, seabirds circling above. captured with an IMAX 65mm large-format cinema camera, expansive depth, massive dynamic range, razor-sharp foreground with soft panoramic falloff, ultra-wide cinematic feel, breathtaking sense of scale, dramatic lighting, highly detailed textures in rock, coat fabric, and ocean mist --ar 16:9 --style raw --v 7

TRADITIONAL CAMERA ANGLES

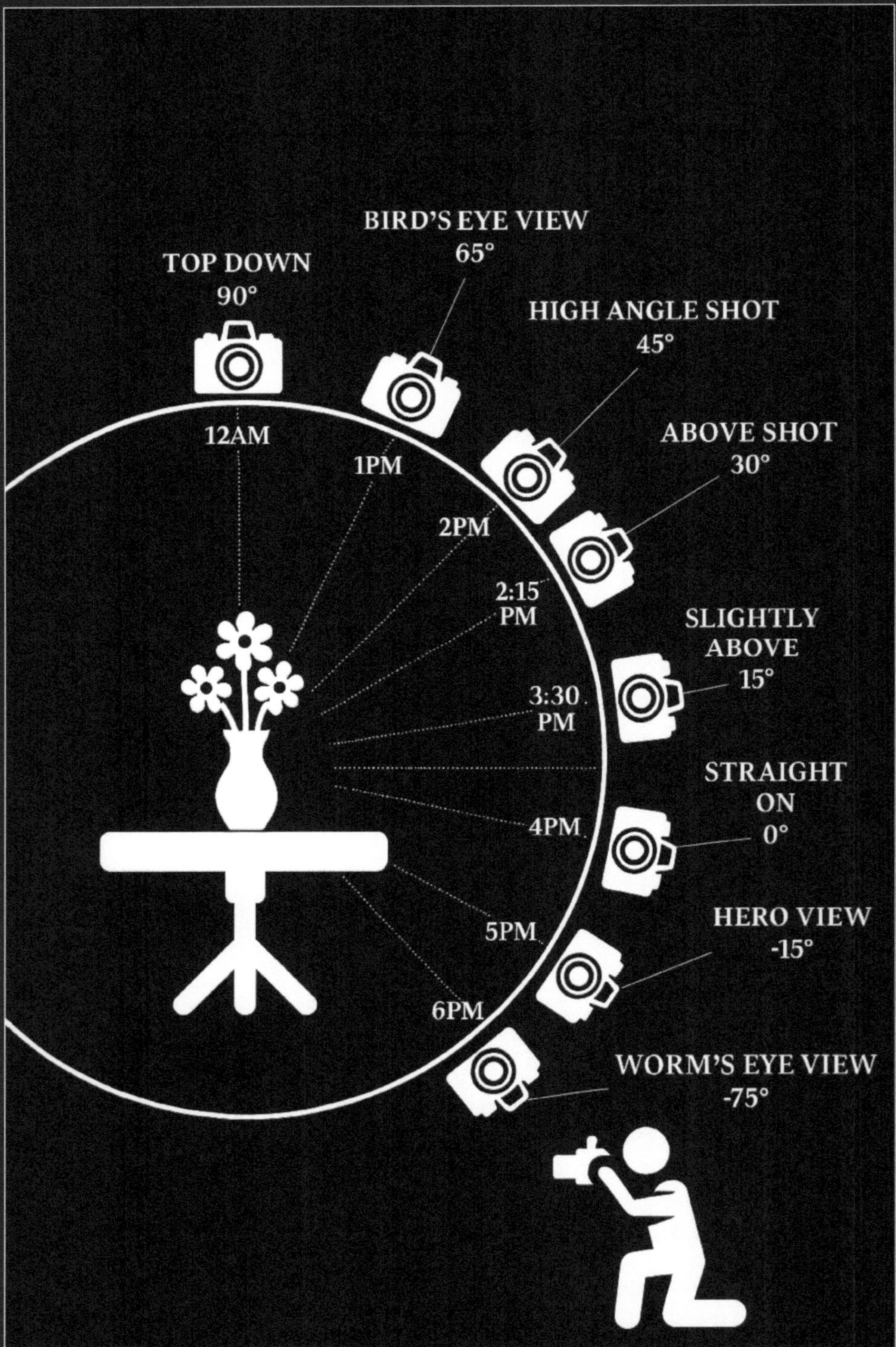

The Art of Camera Angles in AI Cinema

One of the most powerful shifts in AI cinema is how effortlessly we can command complex camera angles. What once required specialized rigs, trained operators, or entire departments can now be achieved through precise prompting. First-person perspectives, extreme fisheye lenses, sweeping crane-style shots, over-the-shoulder reveals, and top-down architectural views—these angles are now instantly accessible with a single line of text. For filmmakers with traditional training, these concepts may feel intuitive. But if you're just beginning your cinematic journey, consider this section your reference guide: a simple, visual way to understand how camera angles shape emotion, storytelling, and the overall impact of your AI-generated scenes. **The following examples will not only highlight each type of shot, but also demonstrate what AI is currently capable of—and the specific text prompts used to achieve these cinematic effects for your AI cinema.**

Camera Angle Examples

Wide Shot	Over-the-Shoulder	High Angle	Tracking Shot
Medium Shot	First-Person POV	Dutch Angle	Top-Down (Bird's Eye View)
Close-Up	Low Angle	Fisheye Lens	Extreme Close-Up

1. Wide Shot

Midjourney Prompt: **cinematic wide establishing shot**, a group of 1990s teenagers hanging out on a quiet suburban street at golden hour, bikes tossed in the grass, cassette player on the curb, long shadows stretching across the pavement, photographed with a Sony Venice 2 capturing the full environment and group dynamic --ar 16:9

Prompt Keyword: **cinematic wide establishing shot**

2. Medium Shot

Midjourney Prompt: **mid-shot framing,** a 1990s teenager leaning against a brick convenience-store wall, backpack covered in band patches, two friends behind him slightly out of focus and clearly separated, warm soda-machine glow illuminating the scene, crisp facial features and clean anatomy, photographed in sharp cinematic realism with the ARRI Alexa Mini LF, high-definition textures, no distortion --ar 16:9

Prompt Keyword: **mid-shot framing**

---

3. Close-Up

Midjourney Prompt: **close-up** of a 1990s teenage girl with butterfly hair clips, freckles catching warm sunlight, blowing a glossy bubblegum bubble, shot with a Canon EOS R5 using a fast portrait lens for rich skin detail and tight emotional focus --ar 16:9

Prompt Keyword: **close-up**

4. Over-the-Shoulder (OTS)

Midjourney Prompt: **narrative over-the-shoulder framing, a** 1990s teenager standing at a sunlit beachside skate park, smiling as he waits with his skateboard under one arm, seen over another teen's shoulder in the foreground, the foreground shoulder softly blurred and taking up the left side of the frame, ocean breeze blowing through palm trees behind him, warm golden light, concrete ramps glowing in the sun, captured in crisp cinematic realism with a RED Komodo --ar 16:9

Prompt Keyword: **narrative over-the-shoulder framing**

---

5. First-Person POV

Midjourney Prompt: **ultra-wide GoPro-style,** a teenager skateboarding down a cul-de-sac, captured from their own viewpoint, looking down at worn Vans sneakers pushing the deck, friends racing ahead, warm sunlight flickering through trees --ar 89:52

Prompt Keyword: **ultra-wide GoPro-Style** or **Immersive First-Person Point-of-View**

6. Low Angle

Midjourney Prompt: **dramatic upward low-angle perspective,** a group of 1990s teens sitting on a jungle gym, photographed from ground level looking up, sky bright behind them, , laces and Converse soles framed in the foreground, captured with a Panasonic GH6 using a dramatic upward angle --ar 16:9

Prompt Keyword: **dramatic upward low-angle perspective**

---

7. High Angle

Midjourney Prompt: **elevated high-angle overhead framing**, 1990s teens sitting in a backyard, playing cards on a blanket, neon water gun tossed aside, snacks spread out, captured from above to emphasize the playful layout, shot with a DJI-style high-vantage viewpoint --ar 16:9

Prompt Keyword: **elevated high-angle overhead framing**

8. Dutch Angle (Tilted Shot)

Midjourney Prompt: **stylized dutch angle,** teens outside a buzzing 1990s arcade, neon reds and blues reflecting off their faces, the camera tilting diagonally for tension and attitude, **the camera is tilted on its roll axis,** so the **horizon line is not parallel with the bottom of the frame**, captured with a Blackmagic Pocket Cinema Camera for vivid color and stylized tilt --ar 16:9

Prompt Keyword: **stylized dutch angle + "the camera is tilted on its roll**

---

9. Fisheye Lens

Midjourney Prompt: **shot with an ultra-wide fisheye lens,** a group of 1990s skater teens goofing around in a parking lot, jeans oversized, chain wallets and stickered skateboards visible, the entire scene bending with exaggerated curvature like '90s skate magazines --ar 16:9

Prompt Keyword: **shot with an ultra-wide fisheye lens**

10. Tracking Shot

Midjourney Prompt: **dynamic cinematic tracking**, a teenager pedaling fast on a chrome BMX, the camera traveling alongside in smooth motion, wheels blurring from speed, warm streaks of sunlight trailing behind, movement, filmed with an ARRI Alexa 65 for sweeping cinematic movement --ar 16:9

Prompt Keyword: **dynamic cinematic tracking**

---

11. Top-Down (Bird's-Eye View)

Midjourney Prompt: **top-down bird's-eye overhead view,** a group of 1990s teens lying on the grass in a circle, swapping stickers and gum wrappers, Polaroids scattered around, , sunlight flickering through tree leaves, captured with a RED Helium 8K from directly above --ar 16:9

Prompt Keyword: **top-down bird's-eye overhead view**

12. Extreme Close-Up

Midjourney Prompt: **extreme close-up** of a child's hand gripping a scratched bicycle handlebar with a torn rubber grip, dusty knuckles, summer sunlight, 1990s suburban childhood, outdoor play nostalgia, shallow depth of field, cinematic realism, film grain, vintage 1970's vibe --ar 16:9

Prompt Keyword: **extreme close-up**

Other Key Terms to Understand

Insert shots

A close or detail shot that emphasizes a specific object, action, or piece of information. Insert shots punctuate a scene and add clarity, tension, or meaning. They are usually tight close-ups—for example, a hand gripping a steering wheel, a phone screen lighting up, or fingers hesitating over a button. Insert shots interrupt a sequence to add emphasis, intention, or emotional weight.

B-roll

B-roll is supplemental footage used to support the main action (often called A-roll). It adds texture, context, and visual breathing room through shots like exterior establishing views, environmental details, crowd reactions, hands at work, or moments of atmosphere without dialogue. B-roll smooths transitions, establishes setting, and creates rhythm, helping a sequence feel intentional rather than rigid. Just to recap the difference: insert shots emphasize a specific detail for meaning, while B-roll provides supporting footage that adds context, texture, and rhythm to the scene.

Cutaways

A cutaway is a shot that briefly cuts away from the main action to another image within the same scene. It helps maintain continuity, smooth edits, or add emotional or narrative context. Examples include cutting from a speaking character to a listener's reaction, a clock on the wall, a detail in the room, or hands fidgeting mid-conversation. Cutaways shape pacing and rhythm, helping a scene flow naturally rather than feeling abrupt or mechanically assembled.

THE VISUAL FORMULA

The Visual Formula & Shot Rhythm

As you begin working with camera angles and different types of shots in AI cinema, it's helpful to remember that cinema is built on rhythm—whether it's made with AI or not. Professional directors rarely place identical shots back-to-back—two close-ups in a row (unless it's a conversation), two wides, or two static angles—because it collapses emotional pacing. Instead, scenes follow a visual formula: wide establishes the world, mid brings us closer to the character, close-up reveals emotion, and insert shots or cutaways add texture and breath to our environment.

This is where many AI creators fall short. As a result, some AI cinema feels flat or repetitive—more like a sequence of "pretty images." Thoughtful shot sequencing ensures your AI-generated story feels intentional, polished, and cinematic rather than randomly assembled. Once you honor the visual formula, every shot supports the next, every scene becomes purposeful, and your AI-generated world gains the intentional pacing of true cinema.

BEGINNER MISTAKES

WHY THIS MATTERS FOR AI CINEMA

Because AI lets you create any shot instantly, many creators unknowingly break the rhythm of cinema, jumping from one striking image to the next without the visual logic or emotional pacing that holds a scene together. AI is so exciting—and the images can look so captivating—that you naturally want to use all of them, but you have to think like the audience. Imagine someone watching your piece with no explanation, no context, and no guidance; the shots have to make emotional sense on their own.

Common Mistakes: Five close-ups in a row. Three wide shots in a row. No B-roll. No reaction shots. No emotional arc. These are the patterns that break cinematic rhythm and make AI-generated scenes feel repetitive, flat, or visually disconnected.

→ "THE BIG RULE"

A common reason AI visuals feel flat is that the same shot type repeats without intention. Cinematic rhythm comes from contrast. When everything is wide, nothing feels intimate. When everything is close, the world disappears. The push and pull of different framing in flow is what creates visual momentum and memorable cinema.

Cinematic rhythm is how you tell the audience what matters. When shots are stacked without variation, nothing is prioritized and the eye has nowhere to rest or anticipate. Contrast creates hierarchy. It guides emotion. It gives the scene shape.

Think like an editor, not a generator. Each image or clip should earn its place by changing how the scene feels or what the audience understands. When rhythm is present, your work stops feeling like a collection of strong frames and starts behaving like cinema—transforming AI visuals from disconnected images into scenes that move a story forward.

Examples

Two mids = visually flat

Two POVs = overstimulation

Two static shots = zero momentum

Two identical framings = story stall

Two wides = emotionally empty

Two close-ups = claustrophobic, unmotivated

Two insert shots = confusing

Two dramatic angles (Dutch/low) = visual noise

EXCEPTIONS TO "THE BIG RULE"

The exception to the rule is intention. Repeating the same shot type back-to-back can be powerful when it serves the moment. Two close-ups can heighten intimacy. Two wides can emphasize isolation. Two mids can anchor a conversation. The difference is not the shot itself, but the purpose behind repeating it. Repetition becomes a form of visual language, signaling time passing, emotional suspension, or a refusal to cut away. Holding the same framing can create tension, discomfort, or calm, depending on what the moment requires. A repeated composition can trap a character inside a feeling, force the audience to sit with something unresolved, or slow time to a near standstill.

However, repetition without awareness feels accidental. The question is not whether you can repeat a shot, but whether the scene demands it. Are you holding because you are uncertain what comes next, or because the stillness strengthens the emotion?

In AI cinema, where generating beautiful frames is easy, it's tempting to sequence images without considering how each shift changes the viewer's emotional position. Cinematic rhythm lives in contrast and control. When repetition is unintentional, the scene stalls. **When it's deliberate, the story moves forward.**

How to Use "The Cinematic Loop" Example

The Cinematic Loop is a practical visual framework for building scenes. Rather than thinking in isolated shots, it helps you sequence images in a way that creates rhythm, emotional progression, and narrative clarity. This section breaks down the camera shots within the loop, along with their meaning and emotional function. You can follow the pattern closely or adapt it to your specific AI cinema needs, but it serves as a strong starting point for understanding how to guide the viewer through moments that feel intentional rather than random—whether you're crafting long-form films, short-form stories, commercials, music videos, trailers, or rapid social media pieces.

Wide Shot → Mid Shot → Close Up → Insert → Reaction → Movement → Wide Shot

1. WIDE SHOT → Establish the world. Introduces where we are, who's present, the mood, and the space. **Emotional function:** *Grounds the viewer. Sets tone. Gives context.*

2. MID SHOT → Brings the viewer closer to the character, revealing body language, movement, and subtle detail. **Emotional function:** *Connects the audience to the character's state without overwhelming.*

3. CLOSE-UP → Reveal emotion. This is where the feeling hits. Eyes, breath, micro-expressions. **Emotional function:** *Creates intimacy, tension, connection, and/or vulnerability.*

4. INSERT SHOT → Add texture or detail.

This is where you paint the picture through detail—hands, objects, a cassette tape, a bike tire spinning, a note being passed, shoes hitting pavement. In these shots, you don't see the character fully. Instead, the focus is on fragments that communicate action, emotion, or meaning without showing the whole. **Emotional function:** *Slows the pacing. Gives the brain something specific and meaningful. In AI cinema, this is where your storytelling begins to feel handcrafted.*

5. REACTION SHOT → Show the response. Reveal how a character absorbs or reacts to what has just occurred. **Emotional function:** *Builds empathy. Creates internal drama. Even silent reactions can change everything.*

6. MOVEMENT SHOT (Tracking / Pan / Tilt) → Shift the energy. A tracking shot, a pan, a tilt — anything that moves the visual language forward. **Emotional function:** *Signals a turn, escalation, or new story beat.*

7. RETURN SHOT (Usually wide or mid) → Reset the space. The camera returns to a re-establishing perspective before the next beat. **Emotional function:** *Reorients the viewer. Prepares them for the next emotional step.*

Additional Shot Pattern Examples

The following examples break down some of the most common shot-pattern formulas used across film, commercials, music videos, and short-form content. These patterns aren't rigid rules — they're proven rhythms that help your scenes feel intentional, emotionally clear, and visually cohesive. Think of them as templates: starting points that give your audience a stable foundation before you begin experimenting with your own style. By understanding how these sequences guide attention, emotion, and pacing, you'll be able to design AI-generated scenes that feel structured and cinematic rather than random or stitched together.

1. The Emotional Punch Pattern

Insert → Close-Up → Extreme Close-Up → Reaction → Close-Up → Mid

This is used to heighten emotions quickly.

Perfect for: arguments, heartbreak, shock, realization, intimate moments, big reveals.

2. The Action Flow Pattern

Wide → Movement → POV → Insert → Reaction → Movement → Wide

It keeps the viewer grounded (wide), energized (movement), immersed (POV), and emotionally connected (reaction).

Perfect for: sports, skateboarding, running, biking, chase scenes, dance.

3. The Suspense / Mystery Pattern

Insert → Insert → Wide → Close-Up → Reaction → Movement

It works because the inserts build curiosity, the wide reorients the viewer, the close-up pulls us into emotional proximity, and the reaction clarifies the meaning. The movement at the end transitions the audience into the next clue or story beat.

Perfect for: thrillers, mystery, or investigative moments.

4. The Comedy Timing Pattern

Wide → Mid → Reaction → Insert → Reaction → Wide

Comedy is built on reactions. This formula creates: setup, anticipation, payoff, beat, reset.

Perfect for: character-driven humor.

5. The Commercial / Branding Pattern

Wide → Close-Up → Insert → Extreme Close-Up → Wide

Why it works: Wide sets lifestyle. Close-up shows product interaction. Insert focuses attention. Extreme close-up sells detail. Wide reinforces brand world. This is the pattern used in 90% of product ads.

Why This Works?

Everything should mirror real human behavior.

You see an object → *Emotion* You get information → *Interpretation* You see Details → *Response*

Conclusion: Cinema mirrors real human perception. We see something, then feel something. We receive information, then interpret it. We notice details, then respond. When these pieces come together, the logic becomes simple: cinema isn't about individual shots—it's about how one shot leads to the next.

The wide shot grounds us in the world. The mid shot connects us to the character. The close-up reveals emotion. The insert draws attention to a detail that signals importance—but meaning doesn't land until we see how that detail is received. This is where the reaction shot matters. The insert shows us what has changed; the reaction shows us what it means to the character. That brief processing moment between the two is the emotional engine beneath the visual formula. Once the character responds, the story can move forward naturally—through action, dialogue, or a shift in mood.

Like any cinematic skill, this rhythm develops with practice. Over time, you'll find your own pacing, variations, and visual instincts. But before breaking rules or experimenting with creative chaos, it's important to master the fundamentals. These patterns give AI cinema structure, coherence, and emotional clarity—and once you understand how they work, you can bend them, stretch them, or reinvent them with intention.

Call to Action

The visual formula mirrors how directors think in shots—moving from space, to emotion, to detail, and back again. But no formula replaces instinct. You still have to experiment and do what feels right so the scene feels intentional rather than assembled. Try This Now: generate one short scene using the Cinematic Loop—**Wide → Mid → Close → Insert → Reaction → Movement → Wide.** Don't aim for perfection. Focus on rhythm. If the sequence feels alive, connected, and easy to follow, you're doing it right.

B-ROLL

B-Roll: Too Much, Not Enough

"Let's keep our story moving forward."

B-roll is both a gift and a trap. Used well, it adds depth, breathing room, and rhythm. Used excessively, it stalls momentum and leaves the audience wondering why they're watching it. In AI filmmaking, this balance is especially tricky because generating beautiful filler shots is effortless. You can create endless cityscapes, landscapes, or moody details in seconds. The real question isn't can you generate them—it's should you use them, and whether they're actually moving the story forward.

B-roll is the supporting footage that fills in around your main shots. Think about what we see before we meet the main character, the front yard before entering the house, hands cooking in a kitchen, or a close-up of an object in the room. B-roll acts as connective tissue, and not every shot needs the character present. Every B-roll shot should either provide new information, establish emotion, or build anticipation for what comes next. If it doesn't, it becomes visual noise. Audiences today—especially on social platforms, have very little patience. A few seconds of wandering B-roll without purpose, and they're gone. AI gives creators unlimited visual material, but knowing where and when to place that material is what separates a forgettable sequence from a story that feels intentional, focused, and easy to follow.

B-roll works best when it's used to:

1. Create emotional contrast between beats.
2. Guide attention toward what matters next.
3. Give the audience time to process before moving on.
4. Establish place or scale before a scene begins.
5. Reveal information without dialogue.
6. Show the passage of time or routine.

Cutaways: Knowing When to Say Goodbye

A cutaway is a type of B-roll shot that briefly cuts away from the main action to show a detail, reaction, object, or environment — then returns to the scene. Examples include a hand turning a key, a crowd reacting, or a neon sign flashing outside before cutting back inside. Cutaways add texture, context, and rhythm when used intentionally. In AI filmmaking, cutaways can quietly take over. You generate one great render, then another, then another — because they're funny, beautiful, or technically impressive. Before you realize it, the edit drifts away from the story and becomes a collection of moments instead of a sequence with direction.

"The story isn't about how many good shots you can include. It's about which shots matter."

This happens constantly in AI cinema because creators feel reluctant to let go of images they love. But storytelling is built on focus, not accumulation. Knowing when to cut a shot — even a great one — is what keeps a piece sharp, coherent, and emotionally grounded. That doesn't mean those shots are wasted. Save them for teasers, social clips, or future projects. But if a shot doesn't serve the story you're telling right now, ***it has to go...***

STYLE

Using Style in Midjourney

One of the most exciting parts of Midjourney is being able to use its style feature. If you've ever watched a Wes Anderson film, you immediately recognize the director's visual fingerprint. The colors, the framing, the textures, the mood—everything feels connected because the style is intentional and consistent. That same level of authorship is now something you can build into your own workflow when making cinema with AI.

Midjourney's style tool lets you create cohesion across images, even when the subject or scene changes. You can write entirely different text prompts or scenarios and apply the same Style Code so the artistic language stays consistent from image to image. Whether you're building a character series, a cinematic sequence, a brand world, or a full visual universe, style becomes the backbone. The Style Code controls the lighting language, color palette, texture behavior, and overall visual logic of the image. In this chapter, we're going to walk through how to use the tool, how to work with Style Codes, how to make your own, and how to maintain visual consistency across everything you create.

Explore Style Codes

To access **Style Code** examples, start on Midjourney's homepage and open the Explorer page from the left navigation, then select the Styles tab at the top. This section contains Midjourney's library of preset styles, each with a Style Code you can view, copy, and paste directly into your prompts. These styles are curated visual identities created by Midjourney and are meant as a starting point—you can use them as-is, modify them, or reference their structure while building your own, allowing you to work with intention and visual consistency rather than guessing what makes a look hold together.

Style Codes

When writing a text prompt, you apply the Style Code at the end of your prompt. Below is an example of what a style prompt code looks like in Midjourney. We will also be going over more examples so you can see how it looks in a prompt.

Example: --sref 3758183124

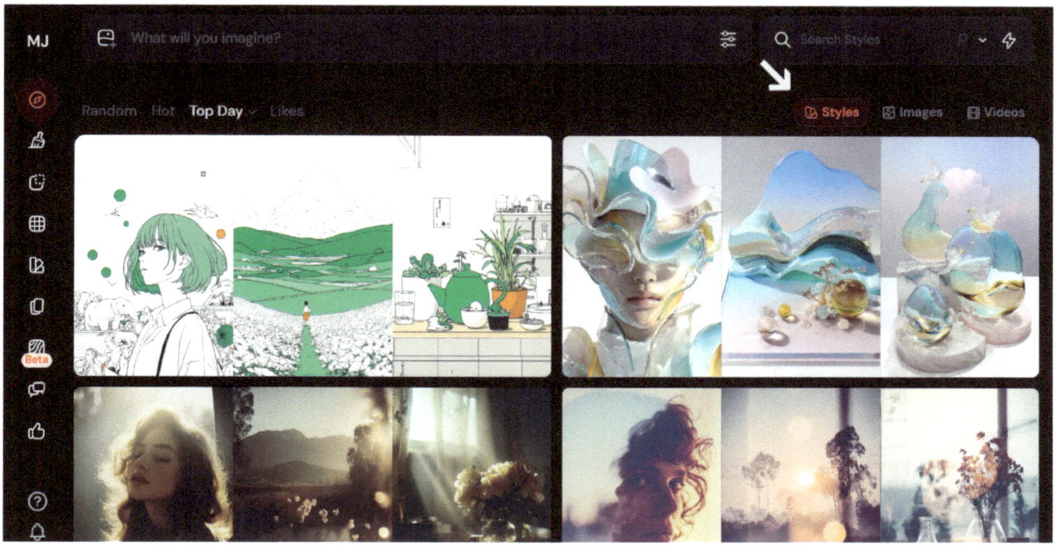

Screenshot as of January 2026

Explore Style Codes

Here is a list of example Style Codes you can use as inspiration or as a starting point to experiment. Each image uses the same text prompt to clearly show how changing only the Style Code affects the result.

Below are the three prompts used across *each set*—feel free to use them if you'd like to follow along.

Midjourney Prompts

1. A portrait of a young person facing the camera, neutral yet expressive gaze, relaxed facial features, natural skin texture, subtle imperfections preserved. The background is simple and uncluttered, allowing full focus on the subject's face. Soft, even lighting with gentle shadows adds depth without dramatization. The composition is centered and intimate, emphasizing presence and character rather than pose. --ar 3:4 --**sref (code)**

2. A still life on a wooden table featuring a bowl of fresh fruit and a simple vase of flowers, balanced composition, natural textures, soft ambient light, subtle shadows, uncluttered background, focus on form and color, quiet observational mood, cinematic realism, gentle depth of field --ar 3:4 --**sref (code)**

3. A group of people walking down a street, captured at street level. The figures move naturally through the frame, creating a sense of everyday motion and rhythm. Buildings and surroundings provide context without overwhelming the subjects. The composition feels candid and grounded, as if observing a moment rather than directing it. --ar 3:4 --**sref (code)**

Style Code Examples

--sref 2342223405

--sref 494951467

--sref 2876533069

--sref 1825292704

--sref 1445349405

--sref 1017427021

--sref 618233246

--sref 459129835

--sref 1478557878

--sref 2298200090

--sref 3089251782

--sref 4229941706

--sref 2945606765

--sref 2755806909

--sref 2790095163

--sref 4221932816

--sref 3171472141

--sref 1429512743

--sref 1170486977

--sref 2744339528

--sref 2930429912

--sref 3702645949

Using an Image as Your Style Reference

Instead of using a generated (--**sref**) Style Code, you can also use an image itself as your style reference. This approach is useful when you're inspired by a specific image and want to use it as a visual starting point rather than working from a predefined style code. In this case, the image becomes the style input, guiding color behavior, texture, lighting, and overall aesthetic direction. To do this, you upload your style reference image directly into the text prompt box by clicking and dragging the image into the prompt field. Midjourney treats that image as a style reference. Please note: Unlike a saved Style Code, this method requires you to include the image each time you run the prompt, since the style is tied to the image itself and not a reusable code.

You can control how strongly the image influences the result using the style weight parameter, written as **(--sw)**, which ranges from 1 to 1000. Lower values allow more freedom from the reference image, while higher values push the result to adhere closely to the image's visual style. One advantage of this method is flexibility—you can include multiple images as style references in a single prompt, allowing you to blend influences and experiment with hybrid aesthetics. This makes image-based style referencing especially useful during exploration, early concepting, or when developing a look from visual inspiration rather than a fixed style system.

Style Reference Example

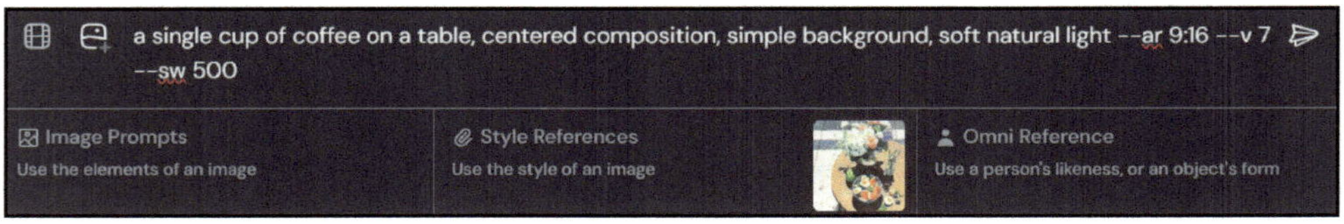

Midjourney Prompt: *a single cup of coffee on a table, centered composition, simple background, soft natural light --ar 9:16 --sw 500*

Results

Style Reference Image

Using the Style Creator (Beta)

The Style Creator is a Midjourney feature designed to help users develop a consistent visual style through visual decision-making rather than written descriptors. Instead of relying on increasingly complex prompt language, it allows creators to guide the model by selecting images that best match their aesthetic intent. You begin with a simple, neutral prompt, and Midjourney generates a range of stylistic variations. By choosing which results feel closest to your vision—based on qualities like lighting, color behavior, texture, realism, or mood—the system gradually learns and refines a cohesive visual language rooted in your preferences.

With each round of selection, variation narrows and consistency strengthens. After several iterations, the style stabilizes and Midjourney generates a reusable Style Code that can be applied to entirely new prompts and scenes while maintaining the same aesthetic identity. This allows creators to separate style from subject matter, enabling experimentation with new compositions, environments, and narratives without losing visual continuity. At its best, the tool reinforces an important creative shift: style is not something you describe—it's something you recognize, choose, and refine through taste and judgment.

Call to Action

Play around! Adding style is so fun. There's something genuinely exciting about seeing a familiar moment reimagined through an artistic lens that feels uniquely yours. Take a moment to build on camera, angles, and the visual formula, and try to create a short sequence in a unique style—whether it's one of the references in this section or a style you create on your own. Style can push a story from something basic and familiar into something memorable. This is the time to play without feeling restricted by structured storytelling, which we'll explore later in the book.

CONSISTENT CHARACTERS

Character Consistency

One of the fastest ways AI-generated work loses credibility is not image quality—it's identity drift. A character looks right in one frame, slightly different in the next, and unfamiliar by the third. The lighting may be beautiful. The composition may be cinematic. But if the audience can't recognize the same person across scenes, the illusion breaks. What you're left with isn't a story—it's a sequence of disconnected images.

The reality is, AI tools are still settling in. Interfaces change, features move, and workflows evolve. With that in mind, this chapter focuses on methods that are repeatable as of today—practical ways to maintain character consistency, including keeping multiple characters consistent within a single scene, using Midjourney and "Google's Nano Banana". While specific interface elements and button locations may change over time, the underlying process remains consistent. The focus here is on learning that process so you can adapt confidently as tools continue to evolve.

Midjourney's Omni Reference

In Midjourney, character consistency is anchored through the Omni Reference, accessed from the dropdown within the text prompt box on the website. You can upload your own image or drag and drop an image you created in Midjourney. This feature allows you to reference an existing image so the system understands who the character is before generating variations according to your prompt. The Omni Reference includes a strength range from 1 to 1000, which controls how strictly the reference image is followed. Lower values allow more variation and reinterpretation, while higher values strongly enforce facial structure, proportions, and identity. A balanced default value is an **Omni Reference value of 100**. You can adjust this value using the sliders in the text prompt or by typing it directly into your prompt using the parameter **--ow** [value].

You may also encounter automatically generated seed numbers in Midjourney, which are used to reproduce similar generation patterns across prompts. Seeds control how randomness is applied, allowing you to revisit or slightly adjust a result rather than starting from scratch. Every generation uses a seed internally, but it is only visible when a result is reused, copied, or shared with its settings intact. While seeds can be useful for refining composition or making controlled variations, they are not required for character consistency. In practice, reference-based workflows are far more reliable for maintaining identity than relying on seed values alone.

→ Establish a Strong Foundation for a Character

Character consistency begins with establishing an initial look. Before prompts or parameters, you need clarity on who your character is—defining features, distinguishing details, and overall visual identity. These decisions shape every image that follows.

Start by committing to a single, intentional reference: a character sheet or, for cinematic work, a clean headshot. This is your foundation. Once you identify the version that feels right, it becomes the anchor for all future generations. Without this step, AI will drift. With it, your character remains recognizable and emotionally consistent across scenes, angles, and tools.

Character Consistency — Example 01

STEP 1: Establish your look

MIDJOURNEY PROMPT: Cinematic portrait headshot of a confident Japanese man in his late 20s with platinum blonde dreadlocks and piercing blue-gray eyes. His face is clearly visible, illuminated with soft, balanced studio lighting that highlights smooth skin and refined facial structure. He wears minimalist gold jewelry and a fitted beige athleisure top, exuding quiet confidence and modern sophistication. Seamless beige background, neutral high-end studio lighting, ultra-luxury wellness and fashion aesthetic, professional actor headshot style, captured on a Hasselblad X2D 100C, 85mm lens, shallow depth of field, cinematic realism, refined composition --ar 16:9

NOTE: Think of creating this headshot and narrowing down your look as an audition—much like casting a film, which, in many ways, you are doing in AI cinema. Feel free to copy this prompt or use it as a template for headshot-style imaging with high detail and controlled lighting.

STEP 2: Use Omni Reference for a New Scene

With your initial character look established, approach each new scene by dragging and dropping the finalized character reference image into Midjourney's Omni Reference box. This anchors the character's identity for each new text prompt.

Begin with a fresh prompt for the new scene. The reference remains constant, while the prompt focuses on what changes—location, action, camera angle, or mood. This separation is intentional: the reference constrains identity while the scene evolves. Note: You must upload the same reference each time for the new scene prompt in order to support continuity across scenes.

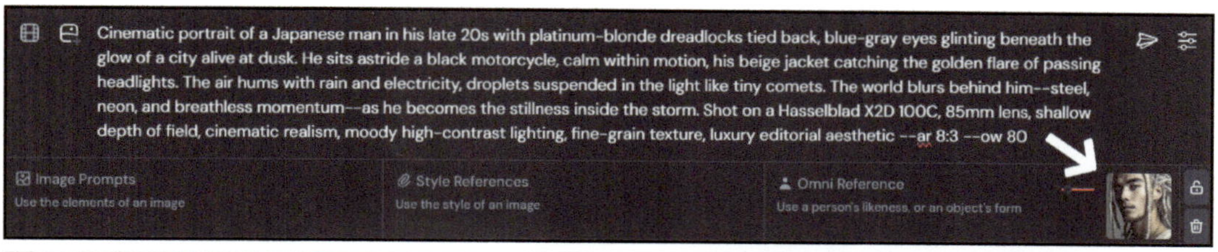

NEW PROMPT WITH OMNI REFERENCE: Cinematic portrait of a Japanese man in his late 20s with platinum blonde dreadlocks tied back, blue-gray eyes glinting beneath the glow of a city alive at dusk. He sits astride a black motorcycle, calm within motion, his beige jacket catching the golden flare of passing headlights. The air hums with rain and electricity, droplets suspended in the light like tiny comets. The world blurs behind him steel, neon, and breathless momentum as he becomes the stillness inside the storm. Shot on a Hasselblad X2D 100C, 85mm lens, shallow depth of field, cinematic realism, moody high-contrast lighting, fine-grain texture, luxury editorial aesthetic --ar 16:9 --ow 200

Using ChatGPT to Generate New Scene Prompts

You can streamline this step by uploading your finalized character reference image into ChatGPT and asking it to help write new Midjourney prompts. When doing so, be explicit: **Ask ChatGPT to restate and preserve the character's defining features in the prompt while describing the new scene.**

This matters because even when using Omni Reference, you want to clearly reinforce facial structure, clothing attire, and any other distinguishing details in the prompt in addition to using the Omni Reference. This helps with the overall appearance in the scene and reduces the risk of drift. The reference anchors identity, but the new text prompt reinforces the intent of the new scene.

Character Consistency — Example 02

STEP 1: Establish Your Look with a Character Sheet

This practice works well for 2D/illustrative and 3D characters.

MIDJOURNEY PROMPT: A stylized Asian woman, in her 20s with large expressive brown eyes, medium-length dark brown hair in a messy bun, warm fair skin with soft subsurface glow, wearing black-and-white striped pajamas, standing confidently in a neutral studio space, full-body character design reference, 3/4 front angle with slight side rotation, arms relaxed, gentle confident expression, cinematic key lighting with soft bounce, clean white-to-neutral gray gradient background, visible fabric texture and realistic skin detail, handcrafted CG aesthetic, stylized proportions (head approximately four times larger than realistic), Pixar-style production character reference render, cinematic realism, high detail 8K --ar 16:9

STEP 2: Use Omni Reference for a New Scene

Results and Corresponding Prompts

1. Midjourney Prompt: A 20s stylized Asian woman with medium-length dark brown hair tied in a loose messy bun, smooth warm fair skin with soft subsurface glow, large expressive brown eyes, delicate facial features, slightly exaggerated proportions with head approximately four times larger than realistic, wearing a green "Starbucks" logo barista apron over a light neutral shirt, standing behind a modern espresso machine, focused yet gentle expression, cinematic natural lighting with warm morning glow, soft volumetric light rays through café windows, gentle contrast, shallow depth of field, realistic materials and fabrics, handcrafted CG aesthetic, stylized cinematic realism, high detail, emotional storytelling composition --ar 9:16 --ow 100

2. Midjourney Prompt: A 20s stylized Asian woman with large expressive brown eyes, warm fair skin, medium-length dark brown hair in a messy bun, wearing black-and-white striped pajamas, standing in her cozy New York apartment kitchen, completely focused as she carefully decorates a small pink cake with white frosting, sunlight streaming through a nearby window, flour and sugar dusted on the counter, a gray cat watching from a stool, cozy clutter of mixing bowls, fruit, and utensils around her, cinematic natural lighting with warm highlights and soft ambient shadows, handcrafted CG aesthetic, stylized proportions (slightly oversized head), CGI-realistic hybrid style, emotional storytelling tone, ultra-detailed 8K cinematic realism --ar 9:16

3. Midjourney Prompt: A 20s stylized Asian woman with large expressive brown eyes, warm fair skin, medium-length dark brown hair in a messy bun, wearing black-and-white striped pajamas, standing barefoot in her cozy New York City apartment hallway near the kitchen, holding a coffee mug, a small gray cat rubbing against her legs, soft morning sunlight filtering through the windows, warm golden light with ambient bounce from kitchen tiles and wooden floor, kitchen visible in background with hanging mugs, fruit bowl, and soft clutter of daily life, cinematic depth of field, handcrafted CG aesthetic, stylized proportions (slightly oversized head), CGI-photoreal hybrid style, cozy emotional tone, storytelling cinematic realism, ultra-detailed 8K render --ar 9:16

4. Midjourney Prompt: A 20s stylized Asian woman with large expressive brown eyes, medium-length dark brown hair in a loose bun, warm fair skin, carrying a beautifully decorated pink three-tier cake with white icing and raspberries on top, walking carefully through a sunny New York City street, wearing elegant business-casual clothing light blouse, beige blazer, and tailored pants, focused but hopeful expression, soft wind moving her hair slightly, yellow taxi and bakery storefronts in background, warm natural sunlight reflecting off glass buildings, cinematic urban depth of field, handcrafted CG aesthetic, stylized proportions (slightly oversized head), CGI-realistic hybrid style, emotional storytelling tone, 8K high-detail cinematic realism --ar 9:16

STRIKE!
MULTIPLE CONSISTENT CHARACTERS

Multiple Consistent Characters in One Scene

At the time of writing, Midjourney does not reliably support placing multiple consistent characters into a single scene. This limitation is largely due to the use of a single Omni Reference slot, which makes it difficult to anchor more than one character identity at a time.

For this reason, the following example demonstrates a multi-character workflow using **Google's Nano Banana.** Because access to Google's Nano Banana continues to shift across platforms, this section uses **Runway AI**, where the integration has remained stable and usable in recent months. While Nano Banana is also available through a growing number of third-party tools, similar to Runway, this book focuses on workflows that have proven reliable over time rather than attempting to document every available integration.

Feel free to explore other third-party options as they become available. The principles demonstrated in this section apply regardless of platform: anchoring character identity, prompting new scenes intentionally, and introducing multiple characters with control.

AI $ubscription for Runway

Runway uses a mix of paid subscription plans and credits—and both can change as new models and features roll out. Even when a plan is labeled "unlimited," not everything is necessarily included without limits. Some tools may be fully available on your plan, while others still rely on credits or have usage caps that shift over time.

The key is setting the right expectations. Start by testing your workflow on a smaller scale so you understand how features consume credits in real use. Once you know what you rely on most, you can choose the plan that fits your process. Because access and structures will continue to evolve, always check current details inside the platform—and build your workflow with flexibility in mind.

How to Access Runway

www.runwayml.com

Runway is a browser-based platform that can be accessed directly through its website with an active account.

Multiple Character Consistency Example

STEP 1: Establish All References

For this example, the character references shown below were created with Midjourney to serve as the foundation for the scene. As a best practice, AI workflows tend to perform more reliably when characters have distinct, clearly defined looks, as stronger visual differentiation reduces ambiguity when multiple characters appear together.

TIP: When designing characters that should feel different but belong to the same world, use a shared style reference (as discussed in the Style chapter, when using Midjourney). A consistent style reference helps unify lighting, texture, and visual language while still allowing each character's identity to remain distinct.

STEP 2: Upload Your Images into Runway

On the Runway website, you will see an option labeled **"App."** Once you are in that interface, click on, **"Models"** then go to **"Nano Banana Pro"** (you may see more than one Nano Banana option—either is acceptable for this workflow). Just note this interface continues to change on Runway, but the tools are still there. This workflow is similar to what you might expect from text-based prompting, but without the parameter hierarchy used in Midjourney; instead, it is more conversational in nature as far as understanding expressive language. For example, be specific without thinking whether it understands or not; for the most part, it will.

Upload Reference Images

Runway Screenshot as of January 2026

Nano Banana Pro: Input Text Prompt

"Put these three characters in a scene. They all are sitting at a fast food restaurant eating burgers and fries. The robot is instead eating bolts and nuts. The burger place is 1980s themed retro with jukebox in the background." Place this in the text box after uploading your images.

Results with Google Nano Banana

Note: From this image, you can download it and upload it into Midjourney to generate video, or generate video directly within Runway. We will explore AI video in its own dedicated section later in the book. As mentioned earlier, clearer and more intentional images lead to clearer video, stronger storytelling, and more cinematic results.

Nano Banana Pro: Realistic People

Nano Banana Pro: Input Text Prompt

"Place both characters together at a casual outdoor picnic. They are seated on a blanket, close to each other, with simple picnic items nearby. The moment feels relaxed and unposed, as if captured during a real interaction rather than staged. Both characters are facing the camera as if they have just looked up mid-moment, not performing for it. Their expressions are soft and natural, with subtle warmth and ease rather than overt smiles. No visible teeth. Their posture is casual and asymmetrical—one leaning slightly forward, the other sitting back more comfortably. The camera is positioned at a three-quarter angle, slightly off-center, creating a candid, observational framing instead of a head-on composition. Lighting is natural and motivated, coming from soft daylight with gentle shadow falloff. Avoid flat, even, or commercial lighting. The overall feeling should be intimate and cinematic, like a quiet moment from a film rather than a promotional image."

**This prompt was written with the assistance of ChatGPT. Feel free to use ChatGPT as a support tool when developing or refining prompts for any platform.*

Results Analysis

As of this writing, maintaining character consistency with realistic human subjects, especially when working with more than one character in a scene, remains more challenging than with illustrative or 3D characters. This is not a limitation of a single tool, but a broader characteristic of how current models interpret realism, anatomy, and identity across generations. The challenge lies in the fact that realistic human features are highly sensitive to small variations—minor shifts in facial structure, proportions, or expression can quickly register as a different person, especially when multiple characters must remain distinct within the same scene.

That said, progress in this area has been significant. While workflows using Nano Banana can still feel experimental when handling two realistic characters—an inherently more complex scenario than single-character consistency—the capabilities in this space are advancing rapidly. Character consistency will be revisited later in the book through select Higgsfield tools, where the focus shifts from static scenes to sequential, story-driven continuation.

Nano Banana Pro: Single Person Testing

Let's jump back for a second to realistic single-person character consistency using Nano Banana via Runway, instead of Midjourney. Below is a quick snapshot of the Runway screen layout, if you're skimming or revisiting this section later. From these examples, Nano Banana proves to be quite reliable for single-character consistency. With that said, Nano Banana results can occasionally feel very clean or polished, while Midjourney may introduce slight facial inconsistencies; however, the overall image can feel more cinematic and poetic. As with all AI tools, these observations reflect the state of the technology at the time of writing and are based on personal testing. Of course, workflows and results may evolve by the time you're reading this.

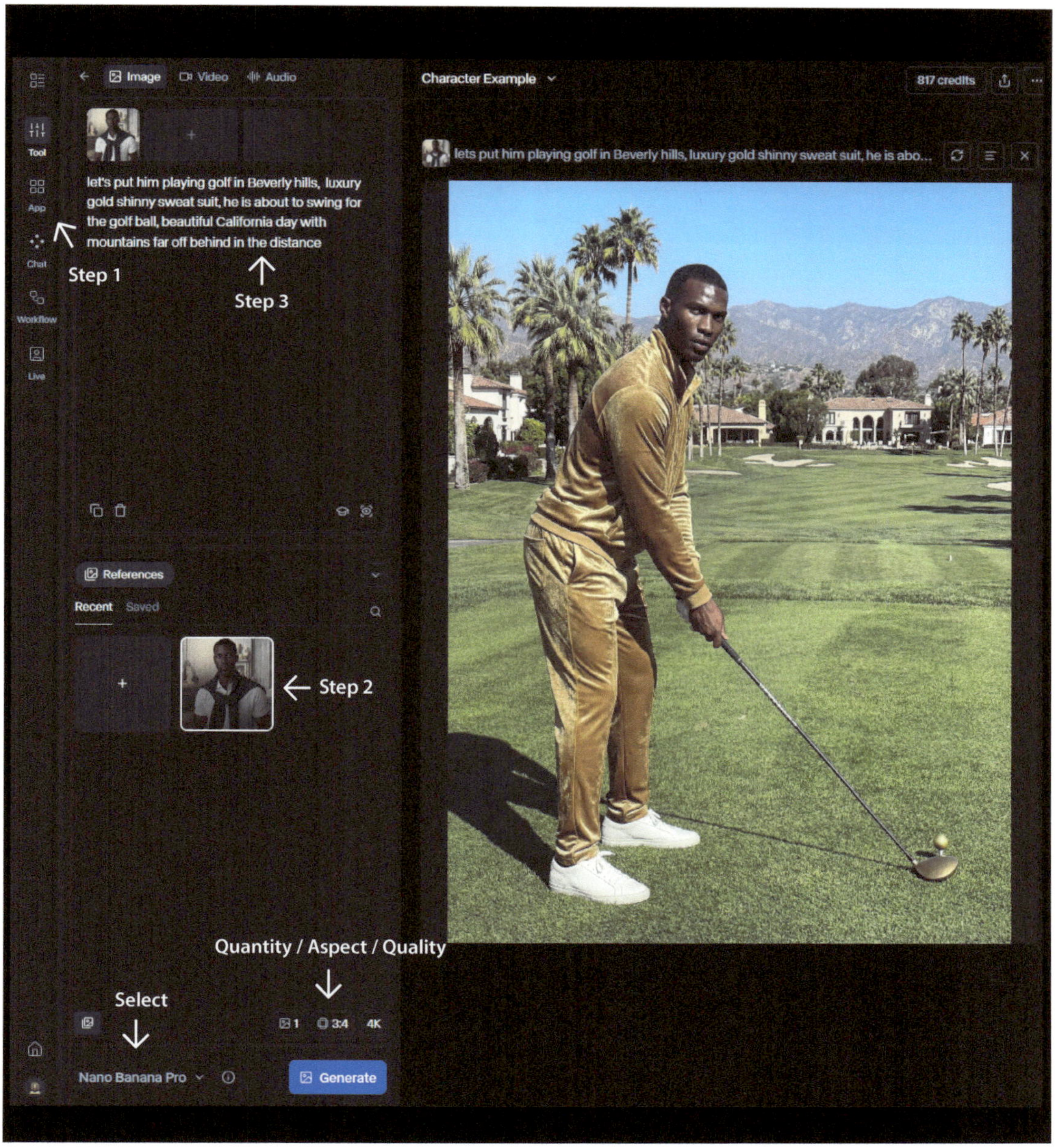

Nano Banana Pro: Single Person

Nano Banana in Photoshop (Brief Note)

Nano Banana has been integrated into Adobe Photoshop–based workflows as part of its Generative Fill–style AI tools, allowing users to experiment with reference-driven generative edits inside a familiar design environment. One advantage of Photoshop-based workflows is the added level of compositional control they offer alongside generation. Tools such as **Generative Fill** and **Generative Expand** can be used to add, remove, or extend elements while preserving visual continuity, and Photoshop's transform and perspective tools make it possible to refine framing or subtly adjust camera angles without regenerating an entire scene. This also opens up the ability to explore the same scene from different camera perspectives, which can be especially useful when testing coverage, mood, or cinematic variation while keeping character identity intact.

Due to the nature of rapidly changing access and interface details, this book does not document Photoshop-specific steps. For readers interested in exploring this workflow further, current tutorials are best found on YouTube, where updates tend to reflect interface changes more quickly. Regardless of platform, the same principles apply: strong references, clear identity constraints, and intentional prompting consistently lead to more reliable results.

Comfy-Based Workflows (Advanced and Optional)

ComfyUI is a node-based interface that provides granular control over image and video generation by exposing each stage of the process—models, references, conditioning, and outputs—as configurable nodes. This structure allows for precise handling of character references, multiple inputs, and complex generation logic that can be difficult to manage through prompt-only interfaces.

ComfyUI itself is free and open source, meaning it can be downloaded and run locally without a subscription or license fee. The primary cost is hardware, as running more advanced or high-resolution workflows typically requires a capable GPU. Some users choose third-party or cloud-hosted versions of Comfy for convenience, which may involve paid plans or usage fees, but these services are optional and separate from the free core software.

One advantage of Comfy-based workflows is the ability to explicitly control how identity, style, and structure are processed, rather than relying on a single prompt pass. This can be valuable for advanced users working on complex scenes, multi-character setups, or repeatable pipelines. However, this level of control comes with a steeper learning curve, requiring familiarity with node graphs and data flow. For these reasons, this book does not document Comfy-specific setups. If you're interested in exploring Comfy-based workflows further, there is a large ecosystem of free tutorials, example graphs, and community resources available on YouTube.

Before we dive into storytelling, I want to pause for a second. You might already have a story in mind—which is great, I love that. But when the ideas start flooding in, when you catch yourself going, *"Oh, I love this idea, and that one, and maybe I should add this too"*—let's slow down and **ask ourselves these three things.**

The below three rules for storytelling are my personal core principles. Hopefully you'll find these rules helpful to return to whenever the momentum picks up and if things start to feel cluttered or bigger than they need to be. It's what I ask myself every time I start and finish a project, in the middle of a project, and before presenting anything. These rules help you strip things back and reconnect with your core. And that is what will make your work successful, notable, and inspiring.

MY THREE RULES FOR STORYTELLING

1. WHY DO WE CARE?

If the audience doesn't care, nothing else matters. Every story requires a core emotional purpose—something that grounds the narrative in meaning. It needs a character we are genuinely invested in, a desire or mission that feels urgent, and stakes that create real tension. Without these elements, even the most visually impressive sequence falls flat. This is the foundation of storytelling: before structure, before style, before spectacle, we must answer one essential question—why do we care?

2. DON'T ASK PERMISSION

If you are trying to convince the audience, you have already lost them. The moment a creator begins begging for approval—over-explaining, over-justifying, or telling instead of showing—the magic breaks. Great stories operate from confidence. They reveal rather than argue, demonstrate rather than defend, and trust the audience to meet them halfway. When a story assumes its own authority, the viewer leans in. When it pleads to be believed, the spell dissolves.

3. MAKE IT CLEAR!

Confusion kills connection. Even though there is always room for anticipation and for the audience to wonder what comes next, they should never be unclear about the fundamentals of a moment: what a character wants, why it matters, or who and what the scene belongs to. Mystery invites curiosity; confusion creates distance. If the audience cannot track the intention driving the scene, emotional investment begins to dissolve. Clarity is not the enemy of depth—it is the foundation of it.

"I want to tell you a story" — here are my story beats

Story beats are the key moments that move a story forward—the small anchors that shape how we experience it. I want to tell you a simple story, and we'll use it as an example throughout this chapter. Sometimes the clearest way to understand storytelling principles is to watch them unfold in real time. After you read the story, we'll walk through why it works—using core principles that apply across many situations. Think of it as a small case study: something concrete we can return to as we talk about clarity, confidence, and how these ideas show up when creating AI cinema.

Story: "Visitors"

1. The Quiet Life

There once was a man who lived in Queens, New York, named Barnabas. He went to work every day and lived a simple and quiet life.

2. The Job

Barnabas worked at a newspaper, writing the obituary section of the paper. One day, a notice landed on his desk about someone who had passed away—and it happened to be a childhood friend of his.

3. The Shock

He was overwhelmed by the news. As he read about his friend's life, he saw the travel and accomplishments laid out on the page. His friend's life looked full and exciting—almost perfect—only to end suddenly in a freak skydiving accident.

4. The Commute Home

On his commute home, he couldn't stop thinking about his friend—their childhood, how they grew up on the same street and how their mothers were best friends.

5. The Night of Doubt

He stayed up all night thinking: Did he make the right choices? He had a 401(k), the same job for twenty years, his bills paid on time... but was that enough? He thought about the trips he never took, the risks he avoided, and how safe his life had become—maybe too safe.

6. Morning Routine

The next morning, Barnabas walked into his usual bodega, keeping to the same routine he always followed before work.

7. An Angel Appears

While looking for his favorite snack for lunch, an angel suddenly appeared beside him.

8. The Reaction

Barnabas froze, completely shocked. He blinked twice, just to make sure he wasn't imagining it. "Who... who are you?" he asked, his voice barely above a whisper. The angel smiled gently and said, "My name is Micah. And yes, you're really seeing me...and only you are seeing me."

9. The Angel's Purpose

The angel said, "I'm in your imagination. I'm here to remind you of the life you're living... and the one you think you're missing." He paused. "Remember how your sister needed help with her kids, and your mother relied on you too. You showed up for them. Your choices shaped more than just your own path."

10. The Reflection

Back at work, Barnabas sat alone in the fluorescent-lit break room, eating his sandwich and thinking about what the angel said. He wasn't sure if it was real or just his imagination, but the message lingered with him.

11. The Weight of the Notice

At his desk, he tried to focus on writing his friend's obituary, but his mind kept drifting. The words felt heavier now. He felt a surge of envy toward his friend's life, even though his friend was gone. The notice just sat on his desk—his friend's photo, that familiar smile—quietly reminding him of everything he couldn't stop thinking about.

12. A Dark Angel Appears

On his commute home that evening, a dark angel appeared. He was leaning casually against the subway station, as if he had been waiting there for him all day.

13. The Whisper

"You know you wasted your life, right?" the angel said to Barnabas. "You played it too small. Your family didn't really need you—you should've looked out for yourself. Your decisions have kept you invisible, and now you're just another tired soul carrying the weight of choices you never made."

14. Torn Between Two Worlds

Barnabas felt uneasy, confused, and split. "What if I really did get it all wrong and my life has just been a waste?" he thought. "I'll be dead like my friend—what will they say about me?" The TV flickered in front of him, but he wasn't really seeing it.

15. The Phone Call

Barnabas received a phone call from his nephew. His nephew told him how much he loved him and how Barnabas had been like a father to him growing up. He shared that he'd just received a huge promotion — and that he and his wife were having a baby boy. For the first time in days, Barnabas felt a quiet wave of relief. He felt happy to be here, in his life, exactly where he was.

How This Story Reflects the Three Rules

Rule 1: Why do we care?

Before anything else, a story needs a character we can understand. Not a perfect character, not a dramatic one—just someone whose inner world feels real. Barnabas works as a starting point because he's relatable. He lives a quiet life, follows a routine, and carries an unspoken question about whether he chose the right path. You don't have to personally live his life to recognize that feeling.

We care about Barnabas because that emotional truth is familiar. The questioning, the comparison, the longing for meaning—these are experiences many people carry, even if they rarely say them out loud. When a character reflects something real back to us, we're invested.

Rule 2: Don't Ask Permission

The story never pauses to convince us it matters. It doesn't justify itself or over-explain. It simply shows us the moments, and we understand them. That's the power of not asking for permission—presenting a story with confidence and letting it land.

That confidence shows up in how the story moves. It doesn't stop to explain what the audience should feel or soften its choices to make sure they're understood. Once a decision is made, the story commits and moves forward. "Don't Ask Permission" means you don't explain the emotion of what you're making, narrate your intent, or defend your choices. You let the story stand on its own—trusting that the audience will meet you there.

Overall, a strong story doesn't ask for attention—it earns it. It pulls you in through clarity, not justification, allowing you to feel immersed rather than instructed. You're invited into the character's world and allowed to experience what's happening without being told how to feel. A strong story never begs—it pulls you in so completely that you forget you ever had a choice.

Rule 3: Make It Clear

A story doesn't need spectacle to make sense—it needs clarity. Clarity in storytelling is about making your message and emotion intentional. Creating a relatable character to drive your storytelling isn't about making someone universally relatable; it's about making their desire and conflict clear.

If we were to sum up this story in one sentence, it would be that Barnabas wants to know if his life meant anything—and that alone is enough. That single emotional anchor allows every other beat—the angel, the dark angel, the friend's obituary, the nephew's phone call—to land with purpose. Without that emotional anchor, it would feel like random things happening with no meaning.

Barnabas's story follows a clean, linear structure: inciting event (his friend's obituary notice) → internal conflict (jealousy of his friend's life) → external voices ("Did I do enough with my own life?") → emotional turning point ("I love my family") → grounding resolution ("I'm happy I was here for this journey"). You always know where you are, what the moment is, and why it matters.

When the audience knows what a character is feeling and why, they stay connected. When they lose track—even for a moment—they disconnect. The story works because there's no guessing game. The purpose of each moment is visible, and clarity in storytelling is what allows everything else to shine, even in a simple, straightforward story like this one.

Of course, different genres introduce complexity in different ways—thrillers, mysteries, dramas, and other layered narratives naturally involve more moving parts. But structure should always be present. The audience needs to know where they are and why it matters. When your story beats follow a purposeful progression, the audience feels guided—they're following a clear journey and are never left guessing or feeling lost.

Where was the B-Roll?

You may have noticed that, in this story example, there is no B-roll—and that was intentional. Before coloring in the smaller details that truly connect an audience to a story and character, it's important to fully understand what the story is about without getting lost in those details too early. Before atmosphere, before style, before cinematic texture, a story needs a solid foundation.

The benefit of building this kind of foundation early is that you can always layer B-roll in later. If you were to add B-roll afterward, you could show, for example, important objects that are meaningful to him in his apartment, whether he has a hobby, or how the world around him feels. You can expand moments and deepen the emotional pacing once the story is clear. If you start adding those elements before the structure is solid, they can become distractions instead of support for your AI cinema filmmaking execution.

The Engines of Storytelling

Every story that works is propelled by a set of fundamental forces. These engines create movement, tension, and audience engagement, shaping how a story unfolds and how it is experienced. When they are in place, a story has direction, pressure, and momentum. Of course, storytelling allows for many variations—different combinations, hybrid structures, and approaches that extend beyond what is highlighted here. This section will focus on some core mechanisms that drive narrative momentum and shape how a story develops.

Core Story Engines Covered in This Section

- Motivation and Mission in Storytelling
- Hero vs. Villain
- High Stakes
- Conflict
- Elements of Surprise

By the end of this section, these engines will give clarity to storytelling decisions —to take your storytelling from beginner to advanced without confusion for yourself or the audience. These elements will make it easier to see what a moment is doing, what it needs to do next, and how tension is built or released through that constant push and pull. With this framework in place, storytelling becomes less about just having amazing story ideas and more about shaping narrative momentum with intention to truly deliver your story in the most impactful way.

> ***"Motivation and Mission*** sit at the center of a story's movement.
> ***Motivation*** moves the story forward***; mission*** determines where it is going."

Motivation — *What Moves a Story Forward*

In storytelling, motivation, in the simplest terms, is the reason a character acts. It is the pressure, desire, fear, or belief that shapes their behavior and pulls them into motion. Motivation turns situations into decisions and gives the audience a way to understand why events unfold the way they do.

Motivation operates on two levels. The first is **core motivation**—the deeper reason a character cares at all. This is the emotional or practical stake that gives the story weight and makes the pursuit matter, such as protecting a village, proving self-worth, or seeking belonging. Core motivation remains relatively consistent throughout the story and explains why smaller actions carry meaning even as circumstances change.

The second level is **situational motivation,** which is the immediate pressure shaping a character's behavior within a specific moment or scene. This is where the deeper drive becomes visible through action. A character might leave a room before a conversation turns personal to protect their identity, or step into a challenge to prove themselves in an unfamiliar space. Situational motivation is how the deeper drive expresses itself in real time as the story unfolds.

Both levels matter. Core motivation gives the story emotional weight, while situational motivation gives it movement and direction. When these layers are aligned, character actions feel intentional rather than random, allowing the audience to follow the story intuitively—whether the stakes involve escaping a mobster or simply deciding when to walk away. Motivation ultimately defines how a character moves through a story.

Mission — What the Story is Organized Around

Mission is the underlying purpose shaping the story as a whole. It is not what the character is trying to achieve in a moment, but what the narrative is designed to move toward. Mission gives the story direction by determining what each scene is building, testing, or revealing. Therefore, mission operates at the story level rather than the character level. A character may be aware of the mission, but the story is not dependent on that awareness. A character may also be unaware of the mission, as it functions independently of the character's intentions, much like moments where the audience understands more than the character does in cinema.

Like motivation, mission operates on more than one level. At its core is the story mission—the central idea or pressure the narrative is organized to explore—it is what ultimately carries the story toward its resolution. This could include testing loyalty, revealing the cost of ambition, or facing a truth.

On another level, mission also becomes visible scene by scene through structural choices. What moments are repeated, what conflicts escalate, what consequences are unavoidable, and where the story ultimately lands are all expressions of mission. These choices determine not just what happens, but why those moments matter in relation to the whole.

The Gap Between Want and Need

One of the most powerful sources of storytelling tension comes from the gap between what a character wants and what they actually need. What a character wants often drives their motivation from scene to scene, shaping their choices and actions. What they need operates at a deeper level, connected to the story's mission and the emotional resolution the narrative is moving toward.

Characters frequently pursue the wrong solution, believing it will resolve the discomfort or pressure they're experiencing. The audience often recognizes the deeper need before the character does, and that awareness creates engagement. We stay invested not just in what the character is chasing, but in whether they will eventually confront what truly needs to change.

This gap generates internal conflict and gives the story its emotional shape. It allows the narrative to evolve naturally, as moment-to-moment motivations collide with deeper truths, without relying on dramatic twists or external spectacle. Over time, the tension between want and need is what carries the story toward its resolution.

Why These Three Matter Together

Motivation, mission, and the gap between want and need work together to give a story movement, direction, and emotional depth. Motivation explains why a character acts in each moment. Mission ensures those actions are building toward something meaningful. The gap between want and need is where tension lives, allowing the story to evolve as the character moves forward before fully understanding what must change. When these three elements are aligned, stories feel intentional, resonant, and complete—driven by character, shaped by purpose, and carried by emotional truth.

Hero vs. Villain in Storytelling

You might be wondering why we're talking about hero versus villain. Outside of genre conventions, this dynamic has nothing to do with costumes, powers, or spectacle. In storytelling, it's simply a way of describing opposition—the force that stands in the way of a character's goal. Sometimes that opposition is an obvious villain. Other times, it isn't a character at all. It can be a looming deadline, an unavoidable consequence, a natural disaster, or a situation with no clean exit. In its simplest form, heroes versus villains is about a character facing a problem they cannot easily escape or solve.

Every story works because something resists the protagonist's goal. That resistance creates conflict, shapes the mission, and clarifies why the pursuit matters. Without opposition, there is no pressure, and without pressure, the story has nothing to push against. At its core, the hero–villain relationship is about ownership and resistance. The protagonist is the character whose desire and decisions move the story forward. The antagonist is not defined by morality, but by function—it is the person, force, or belief actively opposing what the protagonist wants. When this relationship is clear, the audience immediately understands where tension comes from and why the story holds their attention.

The Villain as Circumstances

When thinking about the villain as circumstance, the conflict comes from a situation the character cannot negotiate with, defeat, or escape, which forces difficult choices at times as the story unfolds. A villain as circumstance can take many forms: time running out, a natural event, a system designed with inevitable consequences, or a situation set in motion by past events. Unlike a character villain, a circumstance does not act out of desire or belief—it simply exists. It is the story environment we are sitting in, and its power comes from its indifference.

Villains as circumstance are closely tied to a story's mission. By limiting options and raising stakes, they shape what the narrative is designed to test or reveal. A deadline forces prioritization, a system exposes values or corruption, and an irreversible consequence demands correction. Because a circumstance cannot be confronted or defeated in a battle sense, conflict comes from how the character responds to sustained pressure, which often widens the gap between what they want and what they need. The audience stays engaged not by waiting for a victory, but by watching how the character evolves when faced with a situation that will not change until the story's cinematic ending.

The Villain as a Character

When speaking about a literal character villain, what makes great stories compelling is how closely heroes and villains often mirror one another in backstory. They frequently come from similar places—sharing the same pain, loss, or formative wound. The difference is not the trauma itself, but how each character has responded to it and the results of those choices in forming who they are.

A useful way to understand this distinction is through response and direction. A hero internalizes their experience and looks outward, seeking to prevent others from suffering in the same way. Their motivation turns toward protection, responsibility, or service. A villain responds by turning inward, believing that easing their own pain requires retaliation, control, or diminishing others. Both reactions come from the same source; they simply move in opposite directions.

Seen this way, the hero–villain dynamic is no longer about good versus evil. It becomes a study of motivation, response, and choice. The story's meaning emerges not from what happened to the characters, but from what they decide to do with it. This is why, more often than not, a villain does not see themselves as the villain. From their perspective, their actions feel justified. Their pain feels real. Their response feels validated. They believe they are correcting an injustice, protecting themselves, or finally reclaiming control. That belief is what makes them compelling.

A villain who sees themselves as "evil" is rarely interesting. A villain who believes they are right creates tension, complexity, and emotional weight. Without that internal justification, a villain becomes one-dimensional, and the conflict feels too simple, resulting in audience disengagement.

What is a Hero?

A hero isn't simply defined by being "good," "powerful," or flawless. A hero is defined by how they respond when something pushes back. For this reason, the main character of a story is typically the hero. When a character is faced with opposition—whether it's a villain, a villain of circumstance such as an external situation, or an internal struggle—they are required to continue forward and persevere.

Despite the circumstances, the hero must adjust, endure, and persist. Not because the path is easy, but because stopping would mean surrendering the thing that matters most to them—what they want. The hero's role isn't to eliminate conflict quickly; it's to stay in the fight long enough for the story to mean something. This is why, when watching a film, the creator often pushes the odds so heavily against the hero that winning feels nearly impossible. Challenge after challenge continues to push back, so that when the story finally builds toward victory, it carries real emotional weight for the audience.

What ultimately makes a hero compelling is that they often experience the same doubts, fears, and wounds as the villain. They feel the pull toward self-protection, bitterness, or giving up. The difference is not certainty or strength, but choice. The hero chooses responsibility and movement over stagnation or resentment. Even when unsure, they act. That willingness to keep going under pressure is what sustains engagement. If a hero wins too easily, the story collapses. When they persevere with the odds stacked against them, the journey earns its meaning—and the story stays with the audience.

Why Conflict Keeps the Story Alive

Conflict is the pressure that keeps a story moving. It's what prevents resolution from arriving too easily and forces characters to make choices under stress. Without conflict, there is nothing to push against, and without resistance, a story has no reason to unfold.

One of the clearest examples of this dynamic comes from an unexpected place: professional wrestling. WWE is openly scripted, and audiences know the outcomes are planned. And yet, it remains a billion-dollar industry with fans who stay emotionally invested year after year. The reason isn't the fighting—it's the storytelling. If the hero were to win cleanly every time, the story ends. There's nothing left to root for. So the villain cheats. The rules get bent. The victory is stolen. The hero is pushed back, forced to endure loss, humiliation, or doubt. That resistance is what keeps the story alive. The audience isn't watching to see if the hero will win—they're watching to see how long it takes, what it costs, and whether they can keep going.

This is where many stories fail—they rush the resolution. The villain's role isn't simply to lose; it's to apply pressure long enough for the journey to matter. When opposition disappears too quickly, the story has no time to build emotional weight, and the outcome feels unearned. Across genres and scales, the structure remains the same: a character moves forward, something pushes back, and the story continues because that tension isn't resolved too soon. Conflict doesn't derail a story—it gives progress meaning.

Call to Action

Take a moment to think about the story you're working on. Ask yourself a simple question: what is truly standing in the way of your hero? Not just in terms of external circumstances, but emotionally, too. What pressure keeps the story from resolving too easily? If your hero wins cleanly, the story ends. But if resistance remains, the story stays alive. Look at your villain, conflict, or opposing force and ask whether it's doing enough work. If it isn't pushing back, it isn't serving the story. This is where stronger storytelling begins.

High Stakes in Storytelling

High stakes are not defined only by how big a threat can be, but also by how much your character stands to lose. Explosions down corridors, security guards interrupting a heist, or any other dramatic conflict do not mean anything if there is nothing at risk internally, or if there aren't consequences that extend beyond the moment itself—such as when a smaller mission fails and puts the larger mission at risk of never being completed.

This section will explore why stakes matter in your storytelling and how they can fall flat when your character doesn't change. Flat characters weaken tension even in the most visually impressive cinema. At the core, high stakes are about consequence—what is lost, what is challenged, and who the character becomes when the story's conflict pushes back.

Why Stakes Can Fall Flat

High stakes in storytelling can fail when nothing changes inside the character. A situation can escalate visually, but if new information doesn't alter behavior, the story stalls. This is where characters begin to feel flat—not because they lack personality, but because the story never asks them to choose differently than they would have before. Stakes rise when consequences affect not just the outcome, but the character's internal trajectory.

For example, a character pulls off a heist after heist without ever getting caught. The danger repeats, but nothing truly is at risk. When the character finally gets caught, goes to jail, and later attempts one last job believing it will be their final chance, the stakes rise—because failure now carries lasting consequences. When conflict forces a character to change—whether they make the right or wrong choice—the audience leans in.

Internal vs. External Stakes

Even small stories need stakes—not always explosions or spectacle, but consequence. External stakes describe what happens around a character: what they might lose physically, socially, or materially. Internal stakes describe what happens within them—the beliefs, fears, or sense of self that are challenged under pressure. Strong stories don't choose one over the other; they connect them.

An external event only becomes meaningful when it presses on something internal. Missing a deadline matters when it threatens a character's sense of reliability or self-worth. Losing a job carries weight when it forces a character to confront who they are without that role. A relationship ending matters when it exposes avoidance, regret, or fear of intimacy. Without this connection, events may look dramatic, but they feel hollow.

Emotional stakes are what create engagement. When an external situation challenges how a character sees themselves—or forces them to face a truth they've been avoiding—the conflict becomes personal. Internal stakes give consequence depth, and external stakes give it shape. Together, they turn action into meaning and keep the story moving forward with purpose.

Choice as the Engine of Consequence

Consequence is what gives a story weight, and high stakes are ultimately revealed through choice. A character is forced to decide between outcomes that both cost them something. These moments matter not because of what happens next, but because they expose who the character is becoming under pressure.

Choice is where internal and external stakes collide. External circumstances create the dilemma, but the decision reveals values, priorities, and limits. If a truth does not demand a difficult decision, it won't carry lasting impact. Action alone is not enough—consequence lives in the choice itself, and in how that choice reshapes the character moving forward.

Call to Action

Take a moment to step back and look at the stakes in your story. Ask yourself what your character truly stands to lose—not just externally, but internally. What happens if they fail? What changes if they succeed? Are the stakes forcing your character to confront something real, or are they simply escalating the situation without consequence? High stakes aren't about making the threat bigger; they're about making the outcome matter. When loss, change, and choice are allowed to shape the character, the story gains weight and the tension holds.

Element of Surprise in Storytelling

One of the quickest ways a story loses its effectiveness is when the audience can predict exactly where it's going. When outcomes become obvious, tension dissolves and attention drifts. Storytelling operates through information—who knows what, and when they know it—and surprise emerges from how that information is revealed or withheld.

Elements of surprise are not only about shock or clever twists. They are about control. By shaping the audience's access to information, a story can sustain engagement, redirect expectation, and deepen emotional response. At its core, surprise takes a few distinct narrative forms. Each serves a different purpose. Each creates a different kind of tension. What matters is not using surprise indiscriminately, but choosing the right approach deliberately, at the right moment, to serve the story's intent.

Narrative Configurations of Surprise

A. The audience knows before the character

When the audience knows before the character, tension is created. The viewer is emotionally ahead, watching the character move toward a truth they can't see yet. Every decision becomes charged because the audience understands the risk before the character does. The story lives in anticipation—the waiting, the dread, the hope that the character will realize the truth in time. When that realization finally arrives, the audience feels a sense of release and satisfaction because the moment has been earned.

B. The character knows before the audience

This creates mystery. The character's actions feel intentional, but the reason behind them remains unclear. The audience senses that something is being withheld and is invited to observe, interpret, and piece together the situation rather than being told outright. As a result, this approach depends on restraint, because revealing too much too early collapses the mystery and removes the audience's role in discovery. However, waiting too long risks frustration or disengagement. When handled well, the reveal will feel like closure because the audience was actively involved in uncovering the truth.

C. The audience and the character learn at the same time

When the audience and the character learn at the same time, this creates impact. The revelation is shared, and the emotional response lands strongly because the realization happens collectively. This tactic works best when the audience can recognize that the clues were present all along, but were simply waiting to be understood. When this use of surprise is aligned with the plot (or mission), it creates impact rather than anticipation or mystery. The story clicks into place, and the reveal feels exciting—not just because it was hidden, but because all the elements of the story finally become clear.

Closing Thoughts — *Just Get Started*

Everything in this chapter points to a single truth: story is not something you wait to master before you begin. It's something you understand by layering in these elements—motivation, mission, conflict, stakes, and surprise—and testing how they hold under pressure. Story reveals itself through use.

We're living in a moment where AI makes starting possible immediately. You can test a story beat, sketch a scene, or build a short sequence without permission, without a budget, and without access to traditional gatekeepers. What matters is not how polished the first result is, but whether the story is doing real work—whether something is being pushed, challenged, or revealed.

If you have an idea, you already have enough. Use it. Turn it into a proof of concept. Explore a moment. Add pressure. See what breaks. See what holds. Let the story show you what it needs next. Clarity doesn't come before action—it comes from it.

Every story that lasts begins this way: not fully formed, not perfect, but taken seriously by someone willing to start. Let this chapter be the moment you stop circling ideas and begin shaping one. Start the story, apply the principles, and allow the work to evolve through doing so. Just get started!

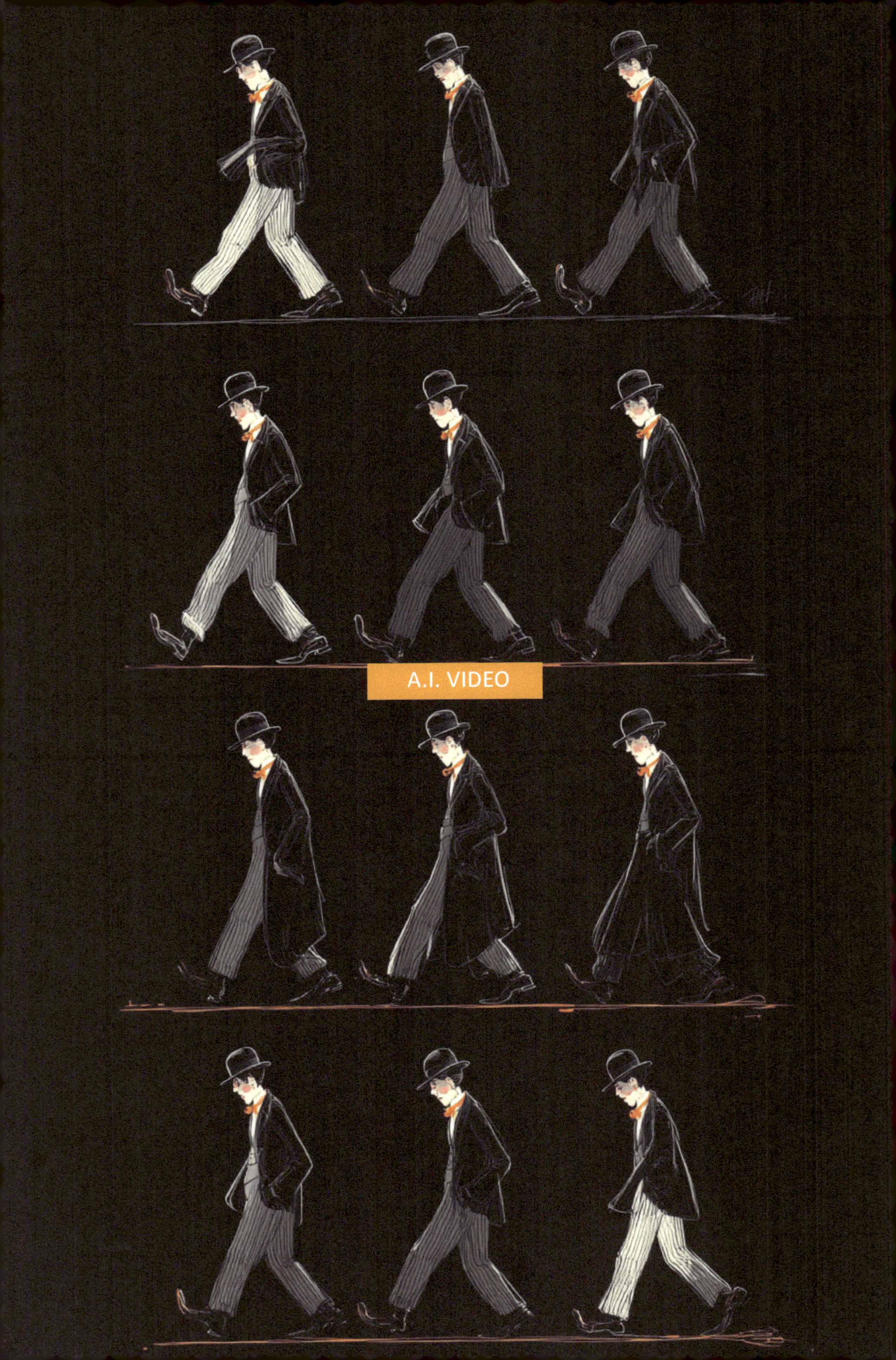
A.I. VIDEO

Introduction for AI Video

From Image → Motion → Cinema

AI video has evolved faster than most people realize. I've been working with these tools since the earliest days, when generating motion that followed basic physical logic was still unreliable. A simple walk cycle couldn't always hold together—characters might step left foot, left foot, left foot, then right, breaking realism immediately. In just a few years, AI video models have advanced at a remarkable pace, with different tools continually competing to improve motion, realism, consistency, and creative control. The underlying logic of movement—how bodies shift weight, how objects interact, and how actions flow from one frame to the next—has continued to improve, though not in a straight line. One month, a tool may produce the strongest results you've seen. A few updates later, another tool may outperform it, or something you relied on for an entire project may suddenly struggle with the next. This uneven progress is part of the current reality of AI video, and learning to adapt is part of the process.

Understanding this landscape doesn't mean subscribing to every tool or chasing every new release. It means staying clear on your goals and open-minded about how you reach them. Different models can produce very different results, and no single platform remains dominant for long. What matters most is your vision and having a clear intention for how the motion, performance, camera, and overall shot should feel. AI assists with execution, but your judgment—deciding which result best serves the story and the completed piece—comes first. The goal is not to become attached to one platform, but to develop a workflow that can evolve as the technology changes. Below is a representative list of AI video platforms and models currently used for generative video.

AI Video Platforms & Models

- Higgsfield (Multi-Model)
- Runway (Multi-Model)
- Midjourney
- Luma Dream Machine
- Google Veo
- OpenAI Sora
- Hailuo AI
- Kling AI
- Adobe Firefly (Multi-Model)
- Magnific Freepik (Multi-Model)
- Pika
- Seedance
- PixVerse
- LTX Studio
- Wan AI

Note: Multi-model platforms provide access to multiple AI tools under a single subscription, allowing you to switch between different approaches to AI video generation while staying on one platform. This makes it easy to test multiple tools in one place, as results may vary.

Using AI to Write Video Prompts

AI language models such as ChatGPT can also be useful for writing and refining video prompts. Instead of starting with a blank page, you can describe the shot you want in plain language and use an AI assistant to organize it into clearer directions for subject action, camera movement, performance, environment, and timing. You can also ask it to tailor the prompt to a specific video model, since a prompt written for Kling may be structured differently from one written for Seedance. This can be especially helpful when developing complex shots or translating a cinematic idea into language that a video model can follow. Rather than keeping up with the preferred prompting style of every tool, you can focus on clarifying your intent, exploring variations, and directing how the story's emotional weight is carried through the performance.

Training Your Eye for Motion

Before working with AI video tools, it's important to train your eye to recognize how motion actually works. AI doesn't invent movement—it attempts to interpret it. The better you understand what makes motion feel believable, intentional, or even when it feels off, the easier it becomes to guide results and evaluate what the tools are producing. This is less about learning AI tools and more about learning *how to see*.

If we look at motion through the lens of traditional animation, it offers a useful way to understand movement because this is how humans originally studied motion in order to recreate it through art—similar to what AI is now attempting to do. A common reference point for animators is what's known as the twelve principles of animation. It's not important to understand all of these principles, but when working with AI video, a few core ideas become especially helpful for training your eye.

AI video will often generate multiple versions of the same footage. Many of them may look similar at first glance, but there is usually one that truly sells the scene. The difference isn't always obvious emotionally—it often comes down to technical cues in the motion itself. Being able to recognize those cues helps you identify which result makes the most sense. Below are few principles to focus on when evaluating motion in AI-generated video.

Principles in Motion

- **Timing and Spacing**
  How fast or slow does the action unfold? Does the motion feel rushed, floaty, or intentional based on how time is distributed across the scene?

- **Weight**
  Does the movement feel grounded and physically believable? Weight shows up in momentum and in how long actions take to resolve, such as moving through water versus running on concrete.

- **Follow-through and Overlapping Action**
  Does motion settle naturally, or does it stop abruptly? Follow-through refers to the main action continuing and resolving naturally, while secondary action describes elements like fabric, hair, or body weight continuing to move and briefly settle after the primary motion. Does this continuation happen, or does everything stop all at once?

- **Arcs and Easing**
  Does the motion follow natural curved paths and ease in and out of actions? Stiff, jittery movement often comes from broken arcs or motion that starts and stops too sharply.

- **Solid form and facial stability**
  Does the character maintain consistent structure, proportions, and facial identity throughout the shot, or does the face distort and drift over time?

- **Appeal**
  Which version feels the most alive? Appeal isn't about perfection—it's about clarity, presence, and whether the motion supports the emotional intention of the scene.

"Plug and Play" | Working Across Multiple AI Video Tools

Rather than walking through every button or interface in each AI video tool, it's more useful to understand the shared patterns they follow. These platforms evolve quickly, and layouts, features, and available models change often. What remains more consistent is the underlying workflow. Depending on the model, you may begin with text, an image, video, audio, or a combination of reference materials. Some tools respond best to detailed direction, while others work better with simpler instructions and strong visual references. The same input can also produce very different results from one model to another. For this reason, AI video is best approached as a "plug-and-play" process: test, observe, and adjust as needed. Over time, you'll discover which tools align with your instincts, pacing preferences, visual style, and the kind of motion you want to create. There is no single "correct" setup, and you don't need to subscribe to everything. This is where multi-model platforms can be especially useful, allowing you to compare different models and approaches within a single workflow.

In the sections that follow, I'll explore prompting techniques for Seedance and creative workflows in Higgsfield, focusing on practical ways to guide motion, performance, camera behavior, and consistency. These are current examples rather than permanent recommendations, as the tools and models available will continue to evolve. Beyond any individual platform, **experimentation is essential.** AI video rewards curiosity, iteration, and trust in your own judgment. The goal is not to become dependent on one tool, but to understand the process well enough that you can adapt as the technology changes. Your workflow will emerge naturally as you play, test, compare, and refine.

Seedance and the Evolving World of AI Video

Seedance is one example of a new generation of AI video models built around improved motion, prompt understanding, cinematic control, and multimodal input. Creators can use text, images, video, audio, or combinations of reference materials to guide a generation. For filmmakers, one of the most practical workflows is **image-to-video.** A carefully designed still image can establish the characters, environment, composition, wardrobe, lighting, and visual style before motion is introduced, creating a clear visual foundation for the shot.

When **creating motion, think like a director** rather than simply asking the AI to "animate" an image. Describe what the subject is doing, how the camera should behave, how characters should move, react, speak, or express emotion, and which elements of the environment should move naturally. For more complex shots, describe actions in chronological order—what happens first, next, and last—to help guide how the scene unfolds over time.

Tip: When a scene involves multiple characters, consider placing them together in a single reference image before generating the video. Establishing their positions, scale, environment, and composition beforehand can help clarify how the scene should come together. Think of it as staging the scene before calling "action" **—the more clearly the setup is established, the less the model has to invent once motion begins.**

Accessing Seedance

Seedance can be accessed through multi-model platforms such as **Higgsfield and Runway,** where it is available alongside other leading AI video models. **There are, of course, many other platforms that offer access, and availability will continue to change as new models and services emerge.** When choosing where to generate, **pay attention to credit usage.** Before beginning a larger project, test your workflow and understand how credits are being used so you can plan your generations efficiently.

Higgsfield AI Video

As mentioned earlier, some platforms provide access to multiple AI models within a single environment rather than requiring you to sign up for individual tools each time. **Higgsfield (www.higgsfield.ai) is one example** of this type of platform. Instead of committing your workflow to a single model, it provides access to a range of AI video models and creative tools that can be tested from one interface. This makes it especially useful for experimentation, since the same idea or starting image can produce very different results depending on the model you choose.

When you first arrive on Higgsfield, the variety of tools and options can feel overwhelming. Many are worth exploring, but you don't need to learn everything at once. Start with the tools that support your immediate creative goal, then expand your workflow as needed. **Different models and generation settings may consume different numbers of credits, and video experimentation can use them quickly. For example, generating in 4K rather than 720p will cost more credits, and generating fifteen seconds of video instead of five will also require more credits.** Test strategically before committing to longer or more expensive generations. Because platforms like Higgsfield evolve rapidly, specific models, features, pricing, and credit requirements will continue to change. As always, I have no affiliation with Higgsfield, and this is not an endorsement of the platform—just a tool I have personally found useful.

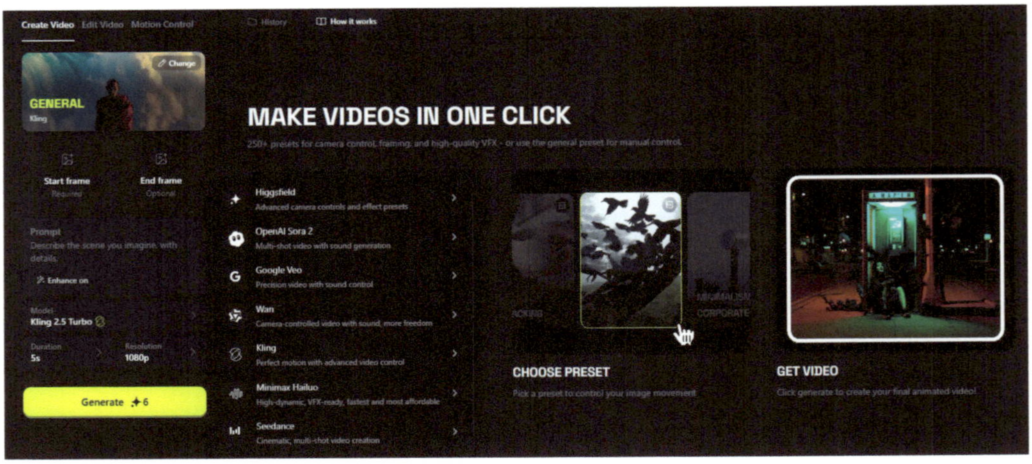

Comparing Video Models

At its core, one of Higgsfield's greatest strengths is the ability to explore and compare different approaches to AI video within one platform. A starting image, reference, or creative idea can be tested across different models to see how each interprets motion, timing, realism, camera behavior, character performance, and continuity. One model may work beautifully for a particular shot while another handles the next shot better. Treat Higgsfield as a creative testing environment: experiment with different models, compare the results, and choose the approach that best supports your vision. The available models will change, but the value of learning how to compare, evaluate, and adapt will remain.

Higgsfield "What's Next" - AI Tool

One of the more notable current developments in Higgsfield is its *What's Next tool.* It allows you to take a single image and have the AI generate what comes after, extending the moment into a continuation that visually complements the original scene. The only current downside—even though things are constantly updating—is that rather than being able to text prompt new scenes specific to your story, the system predicts a possible progression based on the frame you provide. In other words, you do not pick what happens next; the system picks for you. However, there is still so much that can be done; if you keep running it, you can easily piece together a story.

For that reason, I kept this tool in this section rather than the character consistency chapter, because while its ability to maintain a consistent character—even realistic faces—is far more advanced than other AI models at this time, its primary strength lies in continuation. Think of each of these frames as assets you can use to create AI videos, and then, of course, your completed AI cinema. The possibilities are endless.

To access this tool from the Higgsfield home page, navigate to the search tool at the top. Then select **"Apps"** and search for **"What's Next."**

Example of "What's Next Tool" on Higgsfield

Screenshot as of February 2026

Higgsfield "Angles 2.0"

The Angles feature in Higgsfield allows you to generate different camera angles of the same scene, preserving the subject and overall setup while repositioning the point of view. Rather than relying on text prompting or consistent character referencing—which can become fragile and easily collapse under iteration—Angles offers a more stable and predictable approach. At the time of writing, this makes Angles one of the more reliable ways to explore coverage for multi-camera shots within a single AI workflow.

Using a camera rotation control on the right side of the screen, Angles allows you to generate multiple new angles of the same character and setting seamlessly. Currently, you **do** need to reselect the original image before rotating the camera, as the system applies rotation to the modified camera rather than the original image; however, as with all AI tools, this small extra step may evolve sooner rather than later. Overall, this makes the feature especially user-friendly for creators thinking cinematically—for reverse shots, directorial choices such as high angles, mid shots, wides, and more.

To access this tool from the Higgsfield home page, navigate to the search tool at the top. Then select **"Apps"** and search for **"Angles 2.0."**

Example of "Angles 2.0" on Higgsfield

Original Image

→

Generated as of February 2026

Using Motion as a Starting Point

One of the most useful ways to work with AI video is to extract still frames from a generated AI video and reuse them as **new creative assets.** Each AI-generated video is an opportunity to dismantle and reuse as much as possible. A single frame from a video can be upscaled and used as the starting image for a new animation, allowing you to build new motion from a pose or moment that may have been challenging to achieve through text prompting alone. Pulling frames directly from your own video helps the AI maintain visual continuity and intention. This approach also gives you greater control when defining **start and end frames**, since a frame taken from the video can act as a new end frame—helping create a cleaner line of action and clearer direction for the motion in your AI video.

There are several ways to extract a still frame from an AI-generated video, many of which you can find online; however, you can also do this directly in **Adobe Photoshop.** Open Photoshop and drag your video file into the workspace, or use **File → Open** to load it. The video will appear with a timeline at the bottom of the screen. Scrub through the clip until you reach the frame you want, then go to **File → Export → Quick Export as PNG.** Once saved, the image can be upscaled or reused for further editing and animation work. This approach assumes access to Adobe tools, which require a subscription. If you don't have Photoshop, a simple screenshot of the video paused can also work for quick testing, though it will have less control over resolution.

To upscale images, there are several tools available, including Runway AI and Higgsfield. It's also possible to upscale directly in Photoshop using **Image → Generative Upscale.** Not every image captured from video will benefit from upscaling—sometimes the result can introduce pixelation or *artifacts.* Either way, it's important to pay attention to resolution, as it will directly affect the quality and resolution of any new video generated from that image.

LIPSYNC

Introduction to Lip Sync with AI

AI lip sync has advanced dramatically. Spoken dialogue that once required a separate voice track—or often fell completely out of sync with the action—can now be generated far more seamlessly as part of the video itself. Newer AI video models can create characters who speak with synchronized mouth movement, voice consistency, facial expression, and natural pauses within a single generation with the right prompting. The results are not always perfect, but dialogue is becoming less of a technical obstacle and more of a creative decision: How should the character deliver the line, and what should the performance feel like?

One of the most effective ways to guide performance is to **give the AI more context within the image-to-video prompt.** Instead of simply prompting a character to say, "What are you doing here?" explain what has led to that moment and how the line should be delivered. For example, the character may have recently gone through a difficult relationship and has not seen this person in five years following a major fight. They now say, "What are you doing here?" in a somber, curious tone. **Giving the AI a clearer understanding of the character's emotional state can increase your chances of generating a stronger, more believable performance.**

In this section, we'll explore prompting image-to-video scenes with complex dialogue, creating and maintaining character voices with AI voice tools such as ElevenLabs, and improving audio quality so dialogue feels cleaner, more consistent, and better integrated into the final scene.

Prompting Dialogue in Video Generation

When prompting dialogue, it is important to establish each character clearly before introducing the conversation. Define in your prompt who is speaking, how they sound, what they are doing, and how the other characters respond. Present the dialogue and action in a clear sequence so the AI model does not have to guess who speaks next.

For recurring characters, keep the vocal direction consistent across shots by repeating the same core description of age, accent, tone, energy, pacing, and speaking style. Think of this as maintaining a **"voice identity"** in the same way you maintain a character's visual identity.

For more complex shots, it is important to **structure the prompt chronologically with timestamps**—character action, spoken line, reaction, then the next beat. Timestamps can help clarify when each part of the performance should occur rather than asking the AI to interpret everything at once. The overall duration should also be intentional. Before generating, consider how long the dialogue would realistically take to perform. A short line may need only five seconds, while a longer exchange may require ten or fifteen. Giving a generation more time than the scene needs can waste credits, slow the delivery, create awkward pauses, or give the model more room to invent actions or dialogue you did not request. Keep the prompt focused and give the scene only as much time as it actually needs. The following example will demonstrate how these techniques can be applied within an image-to-video prompt.

Image-to-Video Prompting for Complex Dialogue

In preparing your scene for this example, these three character headshots were first created in Midjourney and then combined into a single scene using Nano Banana. **Each character was positioned facing forward in the final image so video models such as Seedance could clearly read their faces before generating the dialogue, camera changes, and alternate angles.** Positioning the characters facing forward should be a part of your prompt when creating your scene image with Nano Banana. AI language models such as ChatGPT can also be a valuable resource for translating your visual intentions into clear prompt language for Nano Banana, particularly when defining character placement, facial visibility, framing, and continuity.

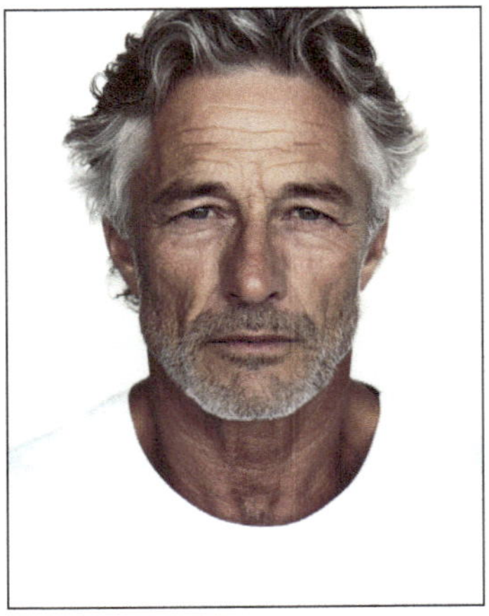

Seedance Workflow Example

Dialogue generation becomes more manageable when the AI model can clearly identify every character before the performance begins. The initial image may look more like a cast lineup than a finished cinematic shot, but that is **intentional.** Its purpose is to give the video model a strong visual reference for all three characters at once. Once camera direction, dialogue, reactions, and timestamps are introduced in the Seedance prompt, the model can create tighter crops, medium shots, and alternate angles based on the original image. Keeping the characters facing forward is especially helpful because their **facial features remain clearly visible.** Profiles, obstructed faces, or characters looking away from the camera give the model less visual information and may make it more difficult to maintain their identities when the scene moves into close-ups.

Below is an example of a prompt you would enter into Seedance when using the prepared scene image as input for image-to-video dialogue generation.

Seedance Prompt

Use the uploaded image as the exact opening frame. Preserve the faces, ages, hairstyles, uniforms, body proportions, and photorealistic identities of all three commanders. Create a fast-paced 15-second science-fiction emergency scene on the command deck. Use clean hard cuts between eye-level close-ups and medium shots. The characters speak quickly and naturally with no long pauses, overlapping dialogue, or additional lines.

Voice identities:
The woman has a clear neutral American voice with controlled urgency.
The middle-aged man has a steady, authoritative American voice with restrained fear.
The older man has a calm, experienced American voice with a measured and confident delivery.

0:00–0:03: Close-up of the woman as warning lights flicker across her face. She says, "The distress signal is ours—sent twelve minutes from now."

0:03–0:06: Hard cut to the middle-aged man at the controls as the ship begins to vibrate. He says, "Navigation is locked. Something is pulling us forward."

0:06–0:09: Close-up of the older man studying the readings. He says calmly, "Reverse the polarity and ride the field outward."

0:09–0:12: Hard cut back to the woman. She turns toward him and says, "If you're wrong, the ship tears apart."

0:12–0:15: Medium shot of all three commanders. The older man answers, "I'm not. Trust the field." The middle-aged man activates the controls as the lighting surges around them.

Additional Workflow Considerations

Of course, this is one technique that can work well for prompting multi-character dialogue, but it is not the only approach. Different scenes, models, and production styles may require different methods. Some filmmakers may begin with a single group image, while others may generate each character's coverage separately and assemble the scene through editing.

When focusing on a consistent voice identity, repeating the same voice description each time can help maintain vocal consistency for each character across multiple shots. However, generated voices may still vary between clips. When greater control is needed, the original voice can be replaced after generation, or the dialogue can be created separately with a tool such as ElevenLabs and applied through a lip-sync or post-production workflow using software such as After Effects. Higgsfield, for example, also includes a "Change Voice" option that can be used after a video is generated to further support voice consistency, where you can upload your voice reference or choose from their voice library.

Ultimately, each project should be approached on a case-by-case basis. Considering the available options and choosing the workflow that best fits the needs of the scene is often the most effective approach.

A.I. Voices

When you see a character on screen — whether it's realistic, 3D animated, or an illustration — there's an immediate sense of identity that comes with it. Matching a voice to that character is almost like a casting call: the voice has to feel native to the visual, as if this person really would sound that way. If the voice doesn't feel right — if it sounds too mechanical, too young or too old, or too "floaty," like it's happening somewhere else and not coming from that character's body — it can throw off an entire project and disconnect the viewer from the world you're building. This is why selecting an AI voice is about more than just generating speech; it's about choosing a performance that feels lived-in and true to the character's presence.

There are a number of capable AI voice tools available — from ElevenLabs and Murf AI to Respeecher and others that offer realistic text-to-speech and expressive voices for different use cases. For the purposes of this book, we'll zoom in on ElevenLabs as a starting point.

Eleven Labs | *www.elevenlabs.io/*

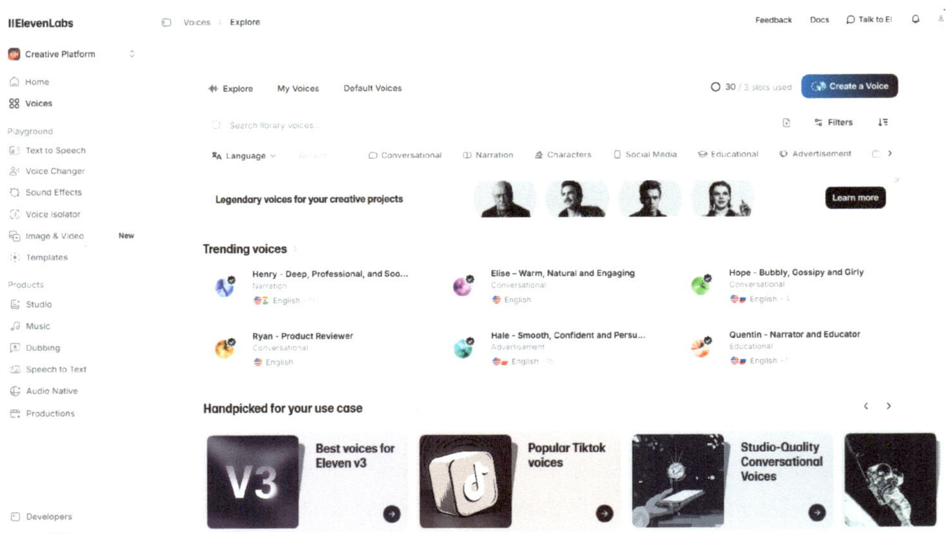

Screenshot as of February 2026

Eleven Labs is often a great starting point for grabbing an AI voice for lip sync because it has an incredible library of voices and speech capabilities that feel natural and *less robotic.* It allows you to generate spoken dialogue that carries rhythm, inflection, and subtle emotional variation—qualities that matter when pairing voices with a character on screen.

At a basic level, ElevenLabs offers a set of free default voices that are immediately usable for testing, narration, and early lip-sync experiments. These voices are clean and reliable, making them a practical entry point when you're just starting out. For more cinematic or conversational needs, like many of these AI tools, a subscription is required to access a more polished, professional, and humanistic quality within the voice library.

Adobe Podcast

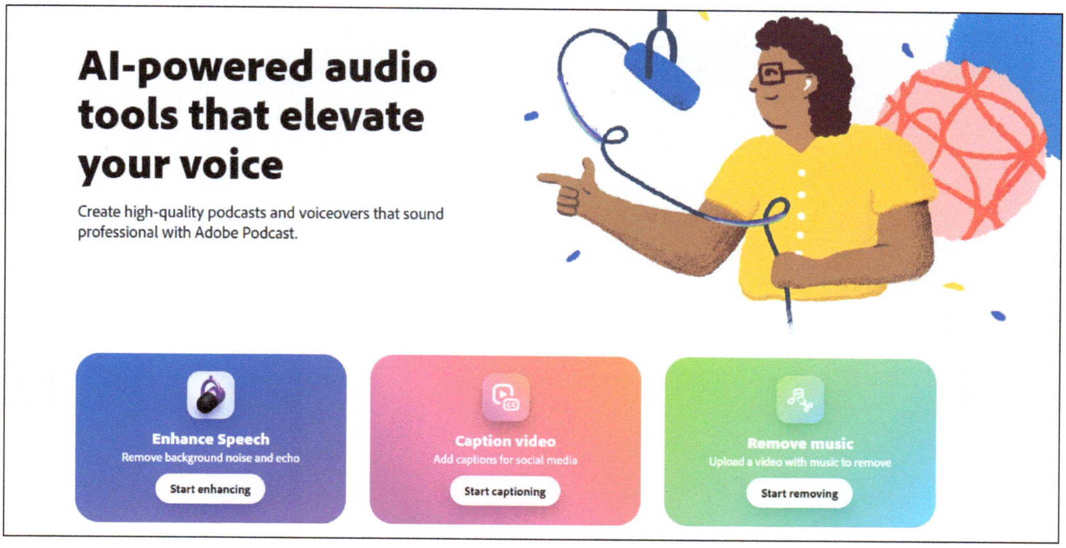

Cleaning Up Audio Quality with AI

A.I.-generated dialogue can sometimes include background noise, echo, music, inconsistent volume, or other audio artifacts. Adobe Podcast provides a simple way to clean and refine these tracks before bringing them into your final edit. Its Enhance Speech feature uses AI to improve vocal clarity, reduce noise and reverb, balance volume, and create a cleaner, more studio-like sound. This can be especially useful when combining dialogue generated across multiple AI video shots, where audio quality may vary from one generation to the next.

Adobe Podcast can also help separate or remove background music from speech, which is useful when an AI video generation produces a strong visual performance and dialogue but includes music you do not want. Premium controls can provide greater flexibility over speech, music, and ambience. As with any automated enhancement, compare the processed audio with the original, since too much cleanup can sometimes remove qualities that made a voice or environment feel natural.

Adobe Podcast offers both free and Premium features. Some advanced options require a paid plan, while access may also be included with certain Adobe Creative Cloud subscriptions. If you already use applications such as Photoshop or After Effects, check what is included with your current Adobe plan, as subscription features and availability may change over time. As noted earlier, I have no affiliation with Adobe; this recommendation is based solely on the tool's usefulness within this workflow.

Call to Action

The best way to understand A.I. dialogue and lip sync is to create a short scene yourself. Start with one or two characters and focus on how voice, facial performance, timing, body language, and framing work together. Direct not only what each character says, but how they say it, keeping voice descriptions consistent across shots. Test different workflows, compare the results, and refine the audio when needed. The goal is not simply perfect lip sync, but a believable performance in which every element supports the same emotional intention.

SOUND DESIGN

How Sound Design Transforms AI Visuals

"The door slams, the floor creaks, your heart is racing"—and nothing has happened yet. That is the power of sound. Our bodies respond because our imagination runs wild with anticipation. You can become so immersed in the moment that you may not even notice that it's the sound—more than the visuals—that's keeping your nervous system on edge.

In traditional filmmaking, sound design is an entire department. In the world of AI—especially if you're a solo creator or planning to become one—sound design becomes essential to understand at a foundational level. If someone takes a sip of coffee in a live-action film, microphones naturally capture that detail on set. In an AI-generated video, that sound may exist; however, AI may not always generate it as intended, and without the specific sounds that match your scene, the moment can feel flat. Understanding sound design will elevate your AI cinema from amateur to professional.

In this chapter, we'll explore how music, foley, and sound effects create emotional timing, anticipation, and meaning. Sound doesn't compete with the image—it supports it, shapes it, and often leads it, guiding how we feel long before a story fully reveals itself. By breaking down the core elements that make sound design cinematic and understanding how they work together, you'll learn to craft sound that doesn't simply accompany AI visuals, but completes them—building mood, emotion, and immersion as part of a unified system. Every story lives twice—once in the image, and once in the sound. The image shows us what's happening. The sound tells us why it matters. That's the invisible language of cinema—and when you understand it, even silence becomes powerful.

The Building Blocks of Sound Design

1. Layering Sounds
2. Fades and Syncing
3. Foreshadowing Impact
4. Dialogue
5. Textures of Sound
6. The Power of Silence
7. Music

Sound is built from a handful of essential elements—layering, foreshadowing impact, fades and syncing, dialogue, textures of sound, the power of silence, and music. Each shapes emotion in its own way, and together they create the rhythm, tension, and atmosphere that define a cinematic experience. In the next section, we'll break down these seven building blocks and show how to use them with intention, so your scenes don't just look cinematic, but feel cinematic—so your sound becomes a beautiful symphony, *not chaotic or off beat.*

1. Layering Sound

Sound design is built as a system of layers. When you combine ambience, foley, dialogue, and music, it's easy to fall into a trap where these elements feel competitive—when in reality, they're meant to complement one another. Every sound file you add should carry its own emotional frequency. For example, when an actor delivers a line, you're not just hearing their voice—you're hearing their breath, the subtle rustle of their clothing, the natural echo of the space, and the low-frequency energy that gives the room its sense of size and weight. Together, these details create depth, realism, and presence. This layering is what turns a flat visual into a living, breathing world—something especially important in AI cinema, since you don't automatically get these natural sound elements the way you would on set. Therefore, you must build them intentionally.

In AI filmmaking, layering becomes even more critical because visuals often emerge extremely clean—polished, surreal, and lacking the kind of realistic grit that comes from real environments. By stacking audio elements with intention, you can create impacts that mark key story beats and further your storytelling into something cinematic and emotionally resonant.

Example: Layering Sound in a Rainy Alleyway

Midjourney Prompt: Pixar-style cinematic rainy neon alley at night, multiple cats walk around the alley, glowing signs in blue, teal, magenta, and amber, wet reflective cobblestone with puddles, soft falling rain, atmospheric mist, richly textured brick walls, scattered crates and posters, pipes dripping water, warm window lights, dramatic color contrast, soft volumetric lighting, highly detailed 3D animated look, whimsical yet moody atmosphere, ultra-clean Pixar rendering --ar 10:3

Imagine you've AI-generated this scene of cats in an alley at night in the city. The visuals might look striking on their own—but without sound, the scene can feel flat, even with perfect animation. **Below is an example of sound design layers you could add to make this shot truly feel alive, using AI tools and free resources.** The resources are summarized on the next page. *Of course, in a full film or commercial, you would think about how each sound blends with the shots before and after—but for this example, we're going to zoom in and treat this as our only shot.*

Sound Layers

1. Ambience (Base Layer)

Ambience is the atmospheric foundation of any scene. For a rainy alleyway, this might include steady rainfall, the soft hum of distant traffic, far-off voices, or faint city echoes bouncing off buildings. This layer creates a sense of place and sets the emotional temperature of the environment. Without ambience, the world feels empty—like a beautiful picture with no life inside it.

2. Foley (Details)

Foley is the art of recreating the everyday sounds we expect to hear, and it's what makes a scene feel physical, textured, and alive. These intimate, grounded details—like water dripping onto metal, the squish of footsteps on wet pavement, clothing shifting as someone moves, or the subtle sounds of the cats themselves—convince the brain that the world on screen exists in three dimensions. Foley brings the physical world to life.

3. Foreshadowing Impact

Impact sounds are the accents of a scene. They mark key beats—like a sudden rumble of thunder, the slam of a distant door, or something shifting deeper in the alley. These moments help guide the viewer's attention and shape the emotional rhythm of the scene. Placed well, a single impact can create tension, surprise, or anticipation.

4. Music (Emotion)

Music is the emotional undercurrent, but not every scene needs it. Even the smallest musical cue can shift the mood—from eerie to tender, from tense to bittersweet. In a nighttime alley scene, subtle musical elements can enhance unease or isolation without overwhelming the natural environment. Used with restraint, music ties the emotional meaning of the moment together.

By layering these elements, the scene transforms from visually interesting to fully cinematic. Play with how sound shapes the moment—let feeling guide the choices. Think of it like composing a song, where ambience, foley, foreshadowing impact, and even music itself work together to build rhythm, tension, and emotional depth.

AI Tools & Royalty-Free Sound Resources

Here's a list of AI and non-AI royalty-free resources to help you achieve professional sound design. Always be sure to check for updates regarding copyright or commercial usage before using any sounds. And of course, you can always record your own foley to bring a personal, tactile touch to your scenes.

Ambience, Impacts, and Foley Sounds

PixaBay
www.pixabay.com/sound-effects

PixaBay has a wide library of ambient tracks—such as rain, traffic, crowd chatter, and room tone—along with foley-style effects like object hits, footsteps, rustling, and basic impacts. It also includes a wide range of urban and nature sounds, as well as background environmental audio. All sound effects are royalty-free with no attribution required, making Pixabay ideal for ambience beds, foundational layers, and general-purpose foley. PixaBay also offers a collection of royalty-free music that can be used for emotional undercurrents or scene building.

Freesound
www.freesound.org

Freesound is a large, crowdsourced library of field recordings, foley, ambient soundscapes, and special effects—ideal when you need unusual or highly realistic textures. Because it's community-driven, each sound has its own license, with some allowing commercial use and others not. Always check the license on the individual sound's page to confirm whether attribution is required or if the sound can be used in commercial projects.

Mixkit
www.mixkit.co

Mixkit offers a clean, easy-to-use collection of sound effects—impacts, swishes, UI sounds, simple ambience, and other quick design elements. It's ideal for fast prototyping, adding small accents, or filling minimal sound design needs. Mixkit's sound effects are free to use for both commercial and non-commercial projects with no attribution required, making it a reliable option when you need straightforward, royalty-free audio.

Sound Bible
www.soundbible.com/

SoundBible is a straightforward archive of sound effects that's quick to browse and download, offering common sounds such as animals, ambient noise, beeps, and mechanical effects. Licensing varies by file—some sounds are cleared for commercial use, while others require attribution or are limited to non-commercial projects—so always check the license listed on each individual sound before using it.

AI and "Royalty Free" Music

Suno AI

www.suno.com

Suno AI can generate full songs, instrumentals, and ambient music from simple text prompts. It's especially useful for creating original music that matches a scene's tone without requiring traditional composition or production skills. Commercial usage is allowed under Suno's licensing, but users should always check for updates or changes to monetization rules, as AI music policies continue to evolve. For custom, royalty-free music, it's a reliable go-to option.

Uppbeat

www.uppbeat.io/

Uppbeat offers a curated library of royalty-free music across cinematic, ambient, electronic, and atmospheric genres. The tracks are clean, modern, and easy to browse, making Uppbeat a strong option for creators who need polished music quickly. Commercial use is allowed, but licensing depends on whether you're using a free or paid plan—free accounts require attribution, while paid plans unlock attribution-free usage. Always confirm the license attached to each track before publishing your project.

YouTube Audio Library

www.youtube.com/audiolibrary

YouTube Audio Library is a widely used resource offering music, ambience, and sound beds at no cost. Many tracks are cleared for commercial use with no attribution required, while others require attribution—each file clearly displays its usage rights. It's a reliable option for fast access to music that's already approved for platforms like YouTube.

Soundraw

soundraw.io

Soundraw creates customizable music tracks that let you adjust mood, length, and intensity. It's especially useful for looping background music or scoring scenes that require precise emotional control. Commercial rights are included with paid plans, while free downloads do not grant permission for commercial use.

Free Music Archive

www.freemusicarchive.org/home

Free Music Archive is a long-running music library spanning indie, experimental, classical, electronic, and atmospheric styles. Licensing varies by track—some are cleared for commercial use, some require attribution, and others are limited to non-commercial projects—so always check the license listed for each track before use.

2. Fades and Syncing

Fades and syncing are invisible but essential techniques. A well-timed fade or sync can carry the audience from one emotional state to another without them consciously noticing—and ideally, they shouldn't. The moment a sound feels abrupt or mistimed, immersion breaks. That's why fades and timing matter so much: they keep sound seamless, natural, and emotionally connected to the image. Subtle crossfades prevent harsh jumps, and even simple elements—like looping rain—benefit from small fades so they don't repeat in a distracting way. Transitions between environments, such as moving from a loud street into a quiet room, feel believable when one ambience fades out as the next fades in.

Syncing is about aligning sound with visuals in a way that feels real rather than rigid. Sometimes the most convincing sync isn't perfectly matched—an impact might land a fraction early for emphasis, or a breath might align with a cut to shape rhythm. For AI creators, this often comes down to sliding sounds slightly forward or backward on the timeline until they *click*. These small adjustments control pacing, energy, and emotional flow. You're not just adding sound—you're shaping how the audience experiences the moment. We'll cover how to apply these techniques in practice in the After Effects chapter.

3. Foreshadowing Impact

Foreshadowing impact is the idea that sound prepares the audience for what's about to happen before the image confirms it. Sound leads perception—shaping expectation, tension, and emotion in advance of the action on screen. A distant rumble, a rising note, or a faint creak can quietly signal change before anything visually shifts. This is one of sound design's most powerful tools, and it's used constantly in professional cinema. In AI filmmaking, this principle is just as crucial: without sound guiding the viewer forward, even striking visuals can feel unanchored. **By placing audio cues ahead of the visual moment, you give the audience emotional direction and momentum—** *because story isn't just what happens next, but what the audience senses is about to happen.*

Example: Foreshadowing Impact — A Locked Door

Imagine a scene where a man stands outside a locked door. He hasn't opened it yet—you haven't shown the audience what's inside—but through sound, you begin to cue the truth. Maybe there's a machine running inside, animals moving around, or people talking. The visuals may be simple, but the audio begins to reveal what the image has yet to show.

Midjourney Prompt: Cinematic shot of a man standing with his back to the camera, facing a closed wooden door in a dim basement or small factory hallway, warm muted tones, soft overhead light casting gentle shadows, textured walls instead of open sky, subtle dust in the air, hints of pipes or old brick, atmosphere quiet and anticipatory as if something is behind the door, emotional storytelling composition, Hasselblad X2D 100C realism --ar 16:9

If a machine is operating behind the door, its presence first shows up as subtle audio hints:

- A faint mechanical hum bleeds through the door, suggesting something active inside.
- Low-frequency pulses build beneath the surface, implying massive power and scale.
- Metallic rattles and sharp electrical crackles cut through the silence, signaling tension and instability, *as if the system is nearing a breaking point.*

By the time the camera finally moves in or the door swings open, the audience already feels the machine's presence. *They have absorbed its atmosphere before ever seeing it.* This is **foreshadowing** through sound in cinema—allowing audio to shape expectation before the visuals catch up. Sound enters first, creating tension in the imagination. The viewer begins constructing the unseen object internally, filling in scale, threat, or significance before the image confirms it.

When the reveal finally arrives, it does not introduce something new—it fulfills something anticipated. The impact lands harder because the audience has already been preparing for it. That is the power of audio-led foreshadowing: **it turns passive viewing into active participation, letting the mind move ahead of the frame.**

4. Dialogue

Dialogue is more than words—*it's the emotional fingerprint of a scene.* The way a line is spoken often tells the audience more than the text itself. In sound design, dialogue becomes a core layer that shapes tone, pacing, and the viewer's connection to the characters. In AI filmmaking, especially with generated voices, dialogue must be handled with intention. The voice carries texture, timing, and subtle imperfections that make the moment feel grounded and real.

Good Dialogue Sound Design Means:

- Clarity without sterility. The audience should understand every word, but the voice should still feel alive—shaped by natural changes in tone, presence, and emotional warmth.
- Placement with purpose. Dialogue doesn't exist in empty space; it lives inside an environment. Adding the right sense of space—like subtle room tone or the natural echo you'd hear in a hallway, kitchen, or open warehouse—helps the voice feel grounded in the world you've created.
- Emotion through performance. A monotone delivery can flatten a scene, no matter how stunning the visuals are. Adjusting pacing, emphasis, or even the pitch of a line can shape how the audience interprets it.

Creating Space for Dialogue

Dialogue must work in relationship with every other sound in the scene. It should never compete with music, ambience, or effects. **When someone speaks, the surrounding audio needs to make room.** Music dips slightly, ambience softens, and effects pull back just enough for the voice to land clearly. This is not simply about lowering volume. *It is about guiding emotional focus.* If the audience has to strain to hear dialogue, their attention shifts away from the story. Creating space around the voice preserves clarity and protects the emotional weight of the line, keeping the viewer connected to the moment. While there are exceptions to every rule, one guideline holds almost universally: *avoid using song lyrics under dialogue.* Lyrics and spoken words compete for the same listening space, often creating confusion even when the music is lowered. Background music without lyrics is generally safe under dialogue and helps support emotion, without competing for attention.

5. Textures of Sound

Not all sound is about ambience or atmosphere—much of what makes a scene feel real comes from texture. **Texture refers to the subtle details and imperfections that give sound dimension:** the grit of vinyl crackle, the difference between footsteps on grass versus pavement, or the dull resonance of a wooden floor. These elements rarely call attention to themselves, but they're what separate flat, artificial sound from audio that feels grounded, lived-in, and professional.

In traditional filmmaking, texture comes from foley and field recordings—wind moving through trees, a buzzing streetlight, distant mechanical noise. In AI cinema, texture is something you build intentionally. Start with a base ambience, then layer in subtle noise: a low hum, a faint rustle, a scrape or vibration that adds friction to the space. *Texture also carries emotional weight.* Clean, airy sounds suggest polish and control, while rough, jagged textures—distorted whispers, crackles, static—create unease and tension. Think of texture as the grain of your soundtrack: it introduces imperfection, scale, and humanity. Without it, even the most beautiful AI-generated scene can feel hollow.

Using Low-Frequency Enhancement

Low-frequency enhancement is the use of deep, subtle bass tones that aren't always heard clearly—*but are felt.* These vibrations work on the subconscious, making a scene feel heavier, more tense, or more powerful. In professional cinema, this energy typically lives in the 20–80 Hz range—the part of the spectrum that tightens your chest during an explosion or makes a space feel like it's vibrating when something massive enters the frame. You don't consciously hear this layer; you experience it physically. A faint low hum can create unease without explanation, while a pulsing bass can make a machine, spacecraft, or reveal feel larger than life by signaling scale before the eye fully understands it.

For AI creators, low-frequency sound is one of the simplest ways to add weight to a scene. An AI-generated image may look stunning, but without a deep mechanical presence beneath it, the moment can still feel flat. Adding subtle sub-bass immediately grounds the scene and gives it physicality. You don't need a professional mixing stage to do this—bass-heavy textures, low rumbles, or sustained tones layered gently under the audio can achieve the effect. Fade them in slowly, pull them back to silence, or let them surge at a reveal. That shift—from quiet pressure to impact—is often when the audience stops just watching and starts feeling the moment.

6. The Power of Silence

Silence is one of the most underestimated tools in sound design. It isn't emptiness—it's tension, focus, and impact. In cinema, silence sharpens the audience's senses, pulling attention fully into the frame and amplifying whatever comes next—or what has just happened.

When sound drops away—the ambience, the music, even the faint background noise—the audience becomes hyper-aware. That pause can heighten suspense, underline a dramatic beat, or create intimacy. Silence before a jump scare makes the impact stronger. Silence before a line of dialogue forces the audience to lean in. In commercials, silence can reset attention, making a reveal or tagline land with clarity and weight.

Professional mixers treat silence as part of the rhythm of a scene. Layers of sound may build—music, ambience, foley—only to cut suddenly to nothing, letting absence do the work. For AI filmmakers, *this is just as powerful.* Muting audio for a brief beat before a reveal or transition gives weight to what follows, especially when paired with visuals that hold tension. **Silence isn't the absence of sound—it's a deliberate choice, and in the right moment, it can be the most cinematic one of all.**

7. Music

Music has always been one of the most powerful storytelling tools in cinema. For decades, music licensing was one of the most expensive parts of filmmaking. Securing the rights to a well-known track could cost more than the rest of the production combined. Independent filmmakers often had to compromise—settling for royalty-free stock tracks that felt generic, or risking legal consequences for unlicensed music.

AI has changed that. Tools like **Suno, Uppbeat**, and **Soundraw** now make it possible to generate cinematic scores tailored to your project's mood, tempo, and genre—for free or at a fraction of the cost. While AI-generated music solves major cost and accessibility issues, respecting artists remains essential. If your project can afford original music or licensing, supporting human composers remains an important part of the creative ecosystem. The goal isn't "AI versus artists," but using AI as a collaborator—a tool that fills the gap when budgets are limited, timelines are tight, or experimentation is needed.

Tips for Making Music Work With Sound

Music should never fight for attention unless you intentionally want it to take over. Knowing when music should carry a scene—and when it shouldn't—is one of the most important parts of sound design. Not every moment needs a score, and not every scene benefits from one. When music overwhelms ambience, foley, or dialogue, a scene can unintentionally drift into *"music video"* territory, even when that wasn't the goal.

A strong rule of thumb: when music is meant to lead emotionally, let it lead. Lower or mute other layers—ambience, foley, low-frequency textures—to give the score room to breathe. When dialogue or environmental storytelling takes priority, the music should pull back. **Great sound design is a negotiation between layers, and music is often the most dominant voice in the room.** Treat music like lighting—it directs attention. *Used intentionally, it elevates a moment. Used without restraint, it distracts from it.*

AFTER EFFECTS

Introduction to After Effects

Whether you're a working professional or opening an editing program for the first time, this section is about bringing everything together. We've come too far to stop now. From Text Prompting, Aspect Ratio, Style, Character Consistency, Cameras and Angles, to Visual Formula, Storytelling, AI Video, Lip Sync, and Sound Design—every chapter has been building toward this moment. It would be incomplete to talk about cinematic timing, emotional sound design, and visual polish without offering a real entry point into a professional editing environment.

Adobe offers two primary tools most filmmakers use: **Premiere Pro** and **After Effects.** Both are powerful. You do not need to master both; however, as you work with Adobe tools, you'll begin to notice that many fundamental concepts overlap. Once you learn one, it becomes easier to understand and master others. My expertise lives in After Effects, which is why this book focuses there and why it remains my go-to tool. In my experience, After Effects provides a single, focused workspace with precise control over timing, motion, and composition.

If editing software has ever felt intimidating, that's normal. These tools are dense by design. The goal here is clarity from the beginning—so the process feels approachable, not overwhelming. Think of this section as a starting point: a solid foundation you can build on as you continue exploring and learning through other resources. By the end of this section, you'll know how to bring your shots to life—and that's the most exciting part of why any of this matters: having full production control from start to finish to tell your story. It may be a long ride, but you can do this. **Let's get started.**

How to Access After Effects

To access Adobe After Effects, you'll need an **Adobe Creative Cloud** subscription, as After Effects is available exclusively through Adobe's subscription model. You can choose a plan that fits your needs, whether that's a single-app After Effects plan or a broader Creative Cloud plan that includes additional tools such as Premiere Pro and Photoshop. Adobe also offers a **free trial**, which allows you to explore the software before committing.

After selecting a plan on Adobe's website, **download** the Adobe Creative Cloud desktop app, which serves as the central hub for installing and managing all Adobe software. Once installed, sign in with your Adobe ID, locate After Effects in the app list, and download it from there. The Creative Cloud app will handle installation, updates, and version management, making it easy to keep track of your applications in one place.

Organize Your Files

When I was in grad school—*years and years ago*—one of my first classes taught how to make and structure folders on a computer. My initial reaction was that this was silly. Of course I knew how to make folders and label them. What I didn't realize at the time was how important this would be.

Once you start working on a project and you have an image here and a video there, it becomes **extremely important** to keep everything organized inside one master folder for each project, with subfolders underneath—however you end up constructing them—as long as you know where things are. This isn't just about staying organized; it's especially important for an After Effects workflow.

When you bring files into the program, **After Effects remembers the file pathway. If you later move a file outside of that structure,** After Effects will display an error because the pathway has been broken, and you'll need to relink the file manually. Keeping a clean and clear file structure from the beginning makes everything flow more smoothly later on.

Saving Your Work

You may wonder why we're talking about saving your work when you haven't even made anything yet. The reason is simple: how and where you save your project determines how smoothly everything else unfolds. Saving isn't something you think about at the end—it's something you lock in at the beginning, because your time matters and you'd never want to lose what you've worked on.

In After Effects, every file is called a **project.** To save your work, go to **File → Save,** which updates the current project file exactly as it is. This is the command you'll use throughout your workflow to save the current state of your project as you work. Make sure you are keeping it in the location you've established as your working folder.

When you're about to make a significant change—or want to preserve a specific version of your work—that's when **File → Save As** (or Save a Copy) becomes important. Saving a new version allows you to create clear milestones, so you always know where to return if something stops working or you want to explore a different direction. This is where staying organized helps when clearly naming different numerical versions of your projects, such as v1, v2, and so on.

Using Save As gives you the freedom to experiment without risking a key moment in your progress, while all versions remain linked to the same media files as the project file continues to evolve. Starting with a clear save location inside your project's master folder ensures that After Effects always knows where your files live, makes versioning easier as the work grows, and gives you stability, flexibility, and control before your project grows in complexity.

New Project & Importing Files

As stated in the Saving Your Work section, every file in After Effects is called a project. From the top menu, you can create or access a project by choosing **File → New Project** to start fresh, or **File → Open Project** to continue working on an existing one.

Once your project is open, the next step is bringing your assets into the program. To do this, go to **File → Import → File** and select the media you need to import. This import action brings in all of the media you'll be working with, including video, images, and audio.

All imported files appear in the **Project panel**, which functions as the project's library and organizational hub. This panel holds every asset connected to your project and is the only place After Effects recognizes media as usable. If a file is not imported into the Project panel, it does not exist inside After Effects. You will see a folder symbol at the bottom of the Project panel that allows you to create additional folders for your imported media within After Effects, helping you stay organized. ***Note:** You can also use the shortcut [**cmd + i**] (Mac) or [**ctrl + i**] (Windows) to import files.

Compositions & "Comps in a Comp"

The above symbol represents the **New Composition tool.** You'll find this small button at the bottom of your Project panel, next to the new folder symbol. Clicking it creates a new composition. **Compositions are the foundation of everything you build in After Effects**—your final film exists only because these compositions are created and assembled.

A composition is essentially a container that holds your media files, timeline, layers, and timing all together. Think of compositions like a large crock pot for a multi-layered dish you're making for dinner. You might have your sauce—such as audio and music—working in one pot, your protein—like video or images—in another, and then your pasta—such as dialogue and conversational audio alignment—prepared separately. However, when it comes time to serve the dish, all of these elements are combined into one meal to enjoy. Sometimes everything can be cooked together, and other times the pasta needs to be prepared separately from the sauce.

Bringing this back to compositions, this is where **"Comps in a Comp"** come into play. You can create multiple compositions within a project, each serving a different purpose. Think of each composition as its own crock pot. Whether you're holding a scene, a single shot, or an entire sequence, placing one composition into another allows you to nest and organize work together and build complex projects in a structured way. You can refine a shot inside one composition, then place it into a larger composition that represents a scene or the full edit. **Any changes made inside the smaller composition automatically update everywhere it's used,** keeping your project organized, flexible, and adaptable as your work evolves.

Composition Settings

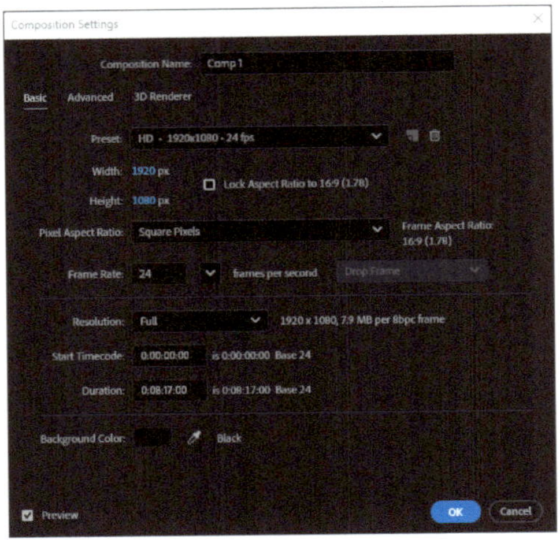

When you create a new composition, you'll be prompted with the **Composition Settings** window. This is where you define the **basic structure of your project** before anything appears on the timeline. Don't let the number of options overwhelm you—*only a few of these settings truly matter at this stage.*

Width and Height determine your resolution and aspect ratio. A common standard is 1920 × 1080, which is HD (16:9) and works well for most horizontal video. If you're working in 4K, the resolution is 3840 × 2160, which offers more detail and flexibility for reframing, but also requires more processing power. For vertical social content—such as Instagram Reels, TikTok, or YouTube Shorts—the standard size is 1080 × 1920 (9:16). **Choosing the correct width and height early ensures your project is framed properly for your intended output and avoids unnecessary cropping or scaling later.**

Frame rate is another important setting. Common frame rates include 24 fps (cinematic), 30 fps (standard video), and 60 fps (smoother motion). **Your composition's frame rate should always match your input media.** To verify this, you can right-click on any imported clip in the Project panel, choose **Interpret Footage → Main,** and check its frame rate. If the frame rate of the video file is 25 fps, change your composition's frame rate to 25. Alternatively, you can convert the video file to 24 fps—either way, the frame rates must match. **Setting this correctly from the beginning keeps motion consistent and prevents playback issues.**

Duration defines how long your composition is, measured in time, and relates to how much space you have on your timeline. It could be just 30 seconds or 10 minutes. Don't worry about getting this perfect right away; **duration can always be adjusted later** as your project evolves, and typically it is. Just start off with enough space on the timeline to get started.

Name your composition at the top of the settings window. This may seem small, but clear naming becomes essential as your project grows and you begin working with multiple compositions.

Composition settings establish the framework for your project, **but they're not permanent.** You can always return and adjust resolution, duration, or other parameters as your needs change. What matters most is that your settings align with your footage—everything else can evolve as the work takes shape.

Workspace

Let's talk about workspace. As you become more familiar with After Effects, this is something you can customize for your own workflow and preferences. However, for the simplicity of this book, we'll work within the Essential Graphics workspace. If you're unsure which workspace you're currently using, navigate to **Window → Workspace → Essential Graphics.**

Timeline & Layers

In the **Essential Graphics** workspace, you will see your timeline at the bottom of the screen. The timeline holds the layers of your media files. **A layer is how your video and audio files appear inside a composition.**

To add a media file to the timeline, **click the file** in your **Project panel** and **drag it onto the timeline.** Once you add more than one media file, you'll see that each file appears as its own **layer.** When layers are stacked on top of one another, **the layer above will visually override any layer beneath it if they overlap on the timeline.** In the timeline, media can be arranged by dragging clips left or right along the track. If you've ever edited in CapCut or Instagram Reels, layers work very similarly here. Media files can be placed side by side to create cuts and sequences—for example, when editing your cinema with mid shots and close-ups that play one after another. Layers can also be stacked on top of each other so they play at the same time, such as when audio and visuals need to play together.

Another essential element of the timeline is the **Current Time Indicator (CTI)**. This is the blue line on the timeline that allows you to scrub through time and view your work at any given moment. **When the CTI is positioned over a media file in the timeline, that frame will be displayed in the viewport.**

Viewport

The viewport, located at the center of your workspace, shows the visual result of everything you've added to the timeline. This is what the viewer will ultimately see in your **final cinematic output.**

As you move the Current Time Indicator (CTI) across the timeline, the viewport updates to display the exact frame at that moment. This allows you to preview timing, framing, and continuity as you build your project. For quick playback, **press the space bar** to play or pause your composition. This shortcut allows you to preview your work instantly without navigating menus, making it easy to check pacing and flow as you go.

Within the viewport, you'll also find a resolution drop-down menu with options such as Full, Half, Quarter, and Third. This setting controls playback quality only—it does not affect your final export. **Lowering the playback resolution can help keep playback smooth as your project becomes heavier with more layers, effects, or high-resolution media.** Overall, the viewport is where your timeline becomes visible, giving you a real-time view of how your project is coming together.

THE TIMELINE IN AFTER EFFECTS

Breaking Down the Timeline

Let's dive deeper into the timeline, because there is a lot to do here. This is where you'll be spending most of your time—*no pun intended.* We'll focus on the essentials, breaking the timeline down through a series of zoomed-in screenshots so each area can be explained clearly without feeling overwhelmed.

Understanding the Time Ruler and Work Area

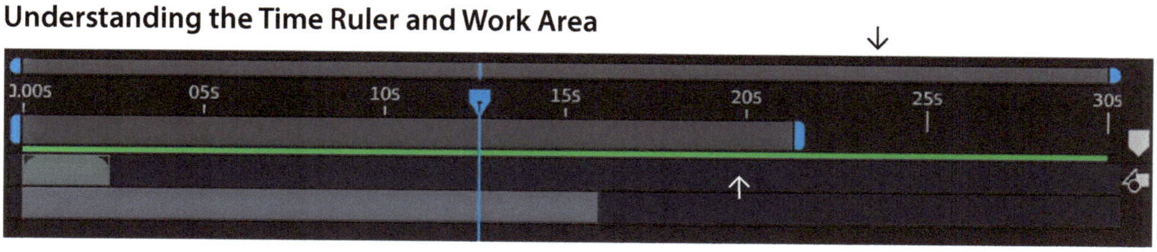

At the top of the timeline, you'll see two horizontal bars that work together to define time in After Effects. The top bar is the **time ruler.** This represents the full duration of your composition from beginning to end, with the numbers indicating time as you move across the timeline. When you slide along the time ruler, you're zooming in and out of different sections of your timeline, letting you see smaller or larger spans of time more clearly. This is especially helpful when lining up media files accurately. Zooming in allows you to make sure media files are staggered correctly without any empty frames as one layer transitions into the next. **Leaving gaps in the timeline between files** will result in random black frames—*even if it's just one frame*—it will disrupt your cinema when exporting your final project. Being able to move through time precisely is important.

The lower bar is your **work area.** The work area highlights a portion of the timeline and defines the range you're currently focusing on for playback. This is commonly used for previewing sections of your project, since render times can be slower when trying to play through an entire five-minute piece, for example, when you may only need to check a 20-second moment. Using the work area allows you to preview smaller sections and drastically speeds up your workflow, so you don't need to play through the entire composition to see how everything is working.

You can slide the work area along the timeline to review smaller sections at a time. It's important to understand that the work area does not limit your project. Your composition can be longer than the work area, and media can exist beyond the work area, extending to the end of the timeline. **The work area is simply a window within the larger timeline.**

Think of it this way:

- The time ruler shows how long your entire project is.
- The work area shows the section you're actively testing in your playback.

Once you recognize the difference between these two bars, the timeline becomes much easier to navigate, and integrate into your workflow.

Adjusting Your Timeline Length

You can adjust your Composition Settings at any time by going to **Composition → Composition Settings.** This allows you to change things like duration, frame rate, or size if you need more time or space on your timeline as your project evolves. You can also use **Composition → Trim Comp to Work Area** to shorten your composition so it matches the visible work area on your timeline. If you later realize you need more time, you can always return to Composition Settings and extend the duration again.

Key Elements of the Timeline

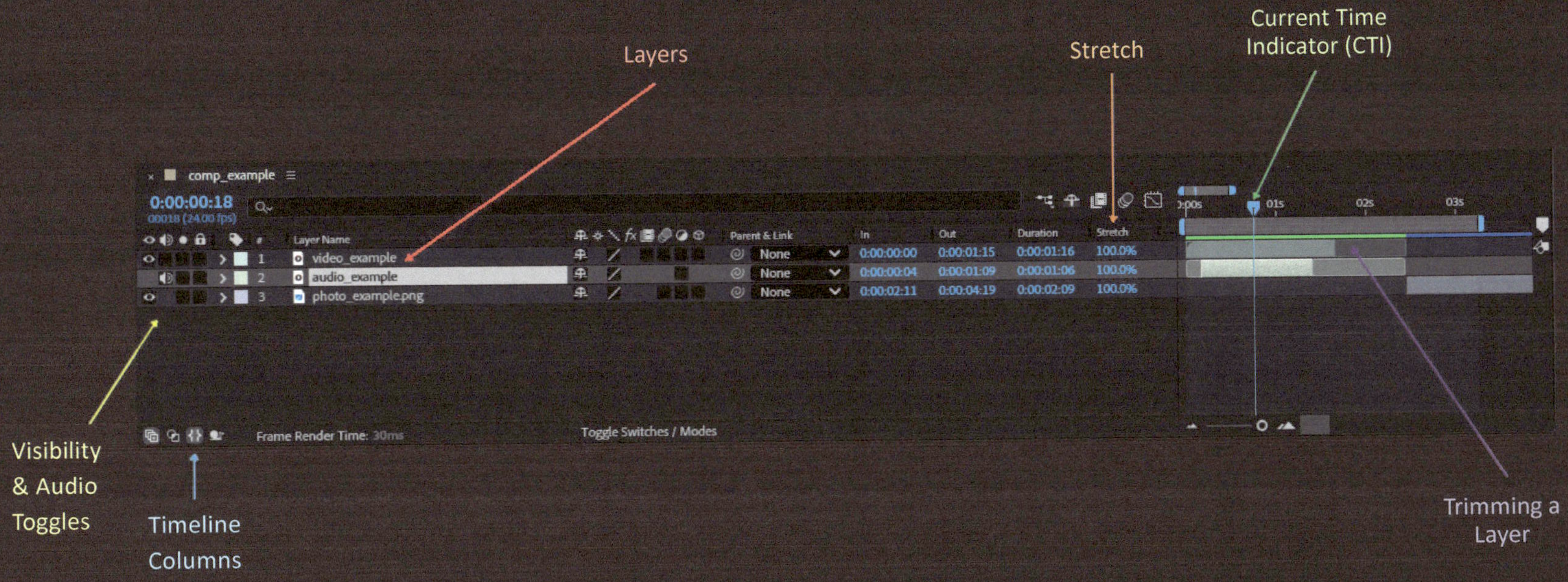

Timeline Columns

The timeline (blue) columns are part of the timeline view. If they are not visible, they can be revealed by clicking the Timeline Columns button (represented by the {} icon) at the bottom of the timeline panel. Once enabled, these columns appear across the timeline, providing the options of In/Out inputs, Duration, and Stretch.

Visibility & Audio Toggles

To the left of each layer name are the visibility and audio toggles.

- The eye icon controls whether a layer is visible in the viewport.
- The speaker icon controls whether the layer's audio can be heard.

These toggles allow you to temporarily hide visuals or mute audio without deleting or altering the layer itself, making it easier to focus on specific elements as you work.

Layers

Just to recap, layers are your media—such as video, audio, or images—and are stacked vertically in this section of the timeline. When layers overlap in time, the order matters visually: layers higher in the stack appear on the screen instead of the layers beneath them. However, when they are staggered, these become your camera cuts.

Stretch

The Stretch value controls the layer's timing for speeding things up or slowing it down. For example, you might use stretch to slow down a moment for emphasis or speed up a clip to tighten pacing. Smaller stretch values speed up your video, and larger number values will slow it down. Entering a negative value—such as -100—will play the layer in reverse, which can be useful for stylistic effects or creative transitions. If you entered -80, the video would play in reverse and be sped up.

Trimming a Layer

When you click on a layer in the timeline, you can trim it by dragging its In Point or Out Point on the layer bar. This controls where a media file starts and ends within the timeline without altering the original file. Once trimmed, only that portion appears in your composition. For video and audio, trimming shows which section of the media plays; for image files, it defines how long the image remains on screen, since still images have no inherent time duration. Trimming is a necessary and useful action when shaping timing, pacing, and cuts within your timeline and compositions.

Current Time Indicator

Reminder: The Current Time Indicator (CTI) is the blue line that moves across the timeline. It shows the exact moment in time you are viewing. Wherever the CTI is positioned is what appears in the viewport, making it essential for previewing playback, aligning layers, and making precise timing adjustments.

Layer Properties, Values & Keyframes

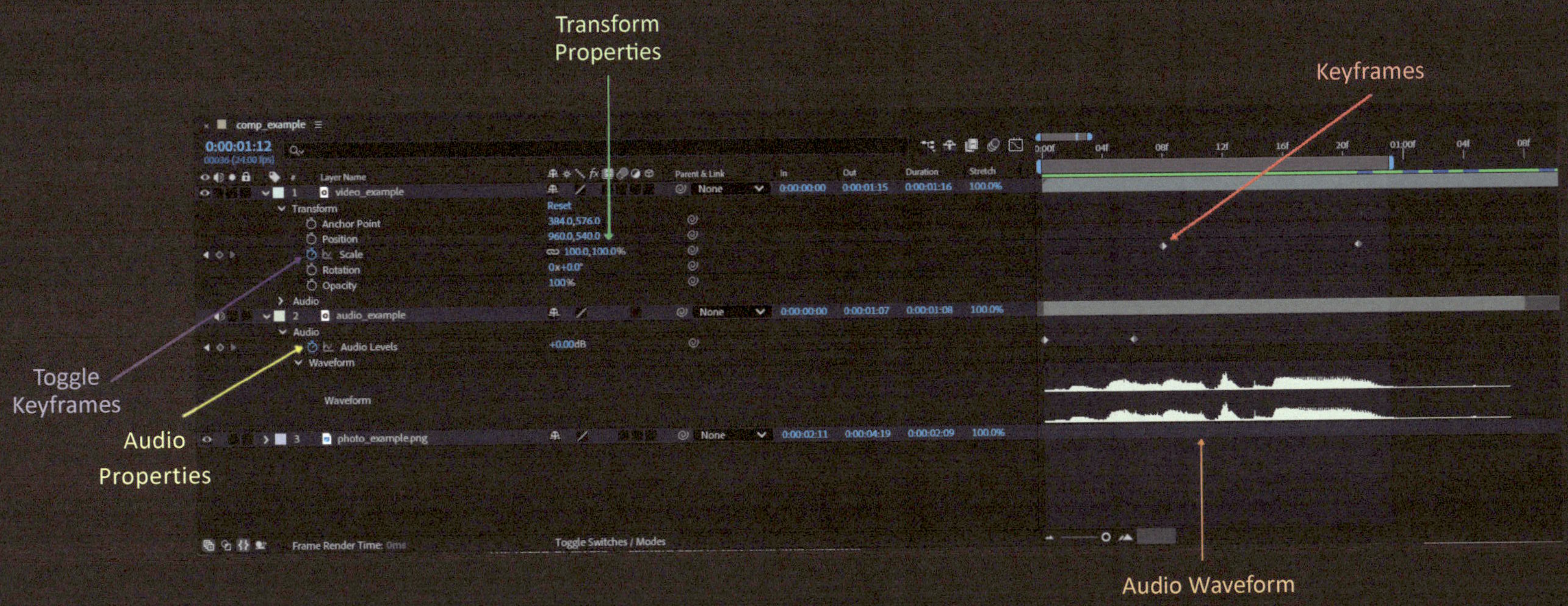

Transform Properties

Each layer contains a set of Transform properties in the dropdown that control how it appears and behaves visually.

These include:

- **Position** – where the layer sits on the screen
- **Scale** – how large or small it appears
- **Rotation** – how much it spins
- **Anchor Point** – the pivot point around which transformations occur
- **Opacity** – how transparent or solid the layer is (fade in/out)

These properties exist on every visual layer—video, images, text, shapes, and even nested compositions. Think of transform properties as the physical controls of your layer. They determine where it is, how big it is, how it moves, and how visible it is at any given moment.

Fun Tip: Fake a Camera Zoom with Scale

You can create the feeling of a camera zoom without changing your AI video by animating the Scale.

For example:

115% → 100% creates a subtle zoom out

100% → 120% creates a zoom in

By keyframing scale over time, you're essentially faking a camera move on a static or AI-generated shot. This works especially well for AI footage, where real camera movement may be limited or unavailable, or when you love the video but it just needs that extra level of polish to really sell the scene. Keep the change small for a cinematic feel. Even a 5–10% scale shift can add life and intention to a shot without feeling obvious. Think of this as giving your frame a breath—a quiet motion that keeps the image or video alive.

Toggle Keyframes / Keyframes

The stopwatch symbol is the **Toggle Keyframe** control. It determines whether a property remains static or changes over time. When the stopwatch is off, the property stays fixed—any value you set becomes a permanent, single state with no movement. When you click the stopwatch, it turns blue, indicating that keyframing is active. From that point on, every adjustment you make to that property is recorded at a specific moment in time. Instead of replacing the value, After Effects stores each change, allowing the property to shift from one state to another as time moves forward. This is what allows motion and gradual change to occur.

Keyframes appear on the timeline as small diamond symbols. Each keyframe marks a specific value at a specific moment in time. By moving keyframes closer together on the timeline, the change between values happens more quickly; spacing them farther apart slows the change down. This distance between keyframes directly controls the timing and feel of motion. You can also right-click on a selected keyframe to access additional options, such as easing in or out, or hold keyframes. While this book won't go deeper into those controls here, there are many online resources available if you want to explore more advanced ways to shape and refine your keyframes.

Audio Properties / Audio Waveform

Audio layers include Audio properties in the dropdown, such as the waveform and access to Audio Levels measured in decibels (dB). The audio waveform provides a visual guide, showing where sound is louder or quieter across time. By keyframing the dB audio levels along the timeline, you can control how sound fades in and out.

For example, setting a keyframe at a lower dB value—such as -50 dB—and gradually moving toward 0 dB (which is the default level), or even a higher value if the audio file is quiet, creates a smooth fade-in. Alternatively, moving from positive dB values down into negative values creates a fade-out. Spacing keyframes farther apart results in a more gradual fade, while placing them closer together creates a quicker transition.

Using both the waveform and keyframed Audio Levels allows you to shape sound intentionally—bringing audio in gently, easing it out cleanly, and avoiding abrupt changes that can break immersion.

Why This Matters in AI Cinema

Transform properties, value fields, toggle keyframes, and keyframes work together to give you control over time. They determine what can change, how much it changes, whether it changes over time, and when those changes occur. Once you understand this system, you're no longer guessing or relying on trial and error—you're making intentional decisions about movement, pacing, and visual rhythm inside your composition.

In AI cinema, this control is essential. AI can generate strong frames, but it does not always decide timing, emphasis, or emotional flow properly. Therefore, being able to speed up, reverse, or scale a video gives you that extra control of believability. This is the point where AI-generated visuals stop being static outputs and begin to function as cinematic work.

Call to Action

Let's pause here for a moment and give yourself time to get familiar with everything we've just talked about. **Open a new project and pull in an image file, two video clips, and an audio file.** They don't need to connect, make sense, or tell a story. This isn't about creating something polished yet—it's simply about exploring.

Click through the timeline. Move layers around. Trim clips. Toggle keyframes on and off. Adjust values. Watch how changes show in the viewport. Take your time noticing what each button does and how the interface responds as you work. This is your space to practice without pressure.

The goal here is familiarity. The more time you spend getting comfortable with the tools now, the less they'll interrupt you later. When it's time to start crafting your cinema, you won't be thinking about where things live or how they work—*you'll already know*. At that point, the tools fade into the background, and your attention can stay where it belongs: on your workflow, your rhythm, and the story you're shaping.

Using Text in After Effects

At the top of the screen, you'll see the toolbar. The symbol with the **T** is the **Text Tool.** Once you select the Text Tool, click and drag directly in the viewport window, and After Effects will automatically create a red text box along with a new text layer. You can change fonts and text settings in the Properties panel on the right side of the screen. If you don't see the Properties panel, navigate to Window → Properties and make sure it is checked.

Just like any other layer, a text layer behaves the same way in the timeline. You can trim its In Point and Out Point to control how long the text appears on the screen. You can also toggle keyframes for Opacity to fade text in and out, scale it up or down, etc.

Think of text layers as tools for film titles, opening cards, end credits, or anything in between—such as captions or on-screen information. Because they behave like any other layer, text layers are incredibly flexible and useful throughout your entire project.

Using Masks in After Effects

Both of these symbols create a mask on a layer. The **Pen Tool** allows you to create a freeform mask, and the **square icon** with a drop-down of other shapes allows for predetermined shape tools. Masks in After Effects allow you to control what part of a layer is visible. For example, you might want to isolate a subject's face, hide an unwanted edge of an image, reveal text gradually, or focus the viewer's attention on one area of the frame without changing the rest of the shot. Masks give you that level of control directly on a layer.

First, select the layer you want to add a mask to, then select one of these tools and click and drag in the viewport window. Once a mask is created, you'll see Mask properties appear under the layer in the timeline. By default, a mask is set to Add, meaning the area inside the shape is visible and everything outside is hidden. Masks can also be set to Subtract, which does the opposite—hiding the area inside the mask while revealing everything around it. You'll also see a Mask Feather option. Mask Feather softens the edges of the mask, creating a gradual transition instead of a hard line. This is especially useful for blending elements naturally, creating subtle vignettes, or making reveals feel more cinematic and less abrupt.

Just like other properties in After Effects, masks can be keyframed. You can toggle keyframes for mask position, shape, feather, or opacity to create reveals, hide parts of an image, or guide the viewer's attention across the frame.

Using Adjustment Layers and Solids

An Adjustment Layer is an empty, invisible layer that holds effects but does not contain any media of its own. To create one, go to **Layer → New → Adjustment Layer**. Adjustment layers allow you to apply effects to everything beneath them in the timeline, rather than to a single layer. They are commonly used for color correction, color grading, blur effects, vignettes, or any global look you want to apply across multiple layers at once. Instead of copying effects onto every clip, you place the adjustment layer above them and apply the effect once. Because it behaves like a normal layer, you can trim its in and out points to control when the effect appears, keyframe its properties, or combine it with masks to affect only specific areas of the frame. Adjustment layers provide a clean, non-destructive way to unify the look of your project and make global changes quickly and intentionally.

Solids are simple layers filled with a single color that can be used in a variety of ways. To create one, go to **Layer → New → Solid.** While a solid may look basic at first, it is one of the most flexible building blocks in After Effects. Solids are often used as backgrounds, color blocks, mattes, or as the base layer for visual effects such as glows, textures, or overlays. Because solids behave like any other layer, they can be masked, scaled, repositioned, and keyframed, including keyframing opacity to fade elements in and out. Like all layers, solids live in the timeline and can be trimmed, layered, and animated over time, making them useful for both subtle polish and more stylized cinematic moments.

Effects and Color Correction

At the top menu of After Effects, you'll find the **Effects tab.** Effects are tools that allow you to modify the appearance, behavior, or quality of a layer. These can include visual changes such as blur, glow, distortion, sharpening, noise, or stylistic treatments, as well as more technical adjustments. Effects are applied directly to individual layers and live inside the Effects panel. While this book does not dive deeply into effects, it's important to know that After Effects offers an extensive library of built-in effects, along with countless tutorials, templates, and presets available online. Many After Effectstemplates rely on pre-built effects, making it easier to achieve polished results while gradually understanding how different tools work together within a professional workflow.

Color correction effects can be found under **Effect → Color Correction** and are used to adjust exposure, contrast, color balance, and overall tone. You can apply color correction directly to individual layers when matching shots or refining specific clips. When working with multiple layers that need a unified look, color correction is often applied using an Adjustment Layer. By adding color correction effects to an adjustment layer and placing it above your footage, the correction affects all layers beneath it. This approach allows you to maintain consistency across your project while keeping your workflow flexible and non-destructive.

→ Let's Make a Movie: Rendering Out Your Cinema

This is the moment where everything you've been building finally becomes a film. Up until now, your work has lived inside timelines, layers, keyframes, and compositions. Rendering is simply the step where After Effects takes all of those elements and turns them into a **single video file—something you can watch, share, and upload.**

What Rendering Actually Is

Rendering is After Effects processing your project—every layer, effect, animation, sound, and timing decision—and packaging it into one playable file. Think of it as exporting the finished version of your work. Your compositions stay exactly as they are; rendering does not change your project. It creates a new file based on what you've already built.

Sending Your Composition to the Render Queue

Before sending your composition to the Render Queue, which is how you will export your project, take a quick moment to confirm two important things.

First, **make sure your Work Area spans the full length of your timeline.** As discussed earlier (see page 125), the Work Area bar defines what portion of your composition is previewed and rendered. If the Work Area only covers part of your timeline, After Effects will render only that section. To export your entire film, drag the Work Area handles so they extend across the full duration of your composition.

Second, check that your viewport playback quality is set back to Full if you previously lowered it to Half, Quarter, or another setting for smoother playback. While lower preview settings are helpful during editing, setting the viewport back to Full ensures you are rendering your project at its highest visual quality before export.

Once those two checks are complete, make sure the composition you want to export is active, then go to **Composition → Add to Render Queue.** This opens the Render Queue panel, where you'll choose your output settings and file destination.

Output Settings (Keep It Simple)

Inside the **Render Queue,** you'll see an **Output Module** section. This determines the format of your final video. For most projects—especially when sharing online, reviewing work, or posting to social platforms—**H.264** is a safe and reliable choice. It produces high-quality video with manageable file sizes and is widely supported across devices and platforms.

You'll also see **Output To,** which lets you choose where the file will be saved on your computer. Make sure this points to your project's master folder so everything stays organized. Once those two settings are in place, you're ready. **Click the Render** button, and After Effects will begin processing your project. Depending on the length of your film, the number of effects used, and your computer's performance, this can take anywhere from a few seconds to several minutes. This is normal. Let it run.

A Note About Exporting

This moment doesn't need to be perfect. *Rendering is not where you solve creative doubts or second-guess your decisions.* It's where you commit to the work as it exists now. You can always revise, re-export, and refine later. **What matters is crossing the threshold from timeline to film.**

Call to Action

Get comfortable. **Don't wait until you're done to do your first render.** The more familiar you are with rendering your work out, the more fluid and confident your workflow becomes. Try rendering small sections as you go—tests, rough passes, even imperfect versions. Let rendering become part of your process, *not a final hurdle.* The goal isn't perfection at this stage; it's familiarity. When rendering feels normal, you're free to focus on storytelling, rhythm, and creative decisions instead of worrying about the technical finish.

Last Thoughts

After Effects may feel unfamiliar at first, and that's completely normal. What you've learned in this chapter is designed to be a solid foundational entry point. You now understand how projects are structured through compositions, how time and layers work together, and how to shape motion, sound, and visuals with intention.

Think of these tools as starting points into a larger creative language. The more you work, the more fluent you'll become—*not by memorizing every feature,* but by knowing where to look, how to experiment, and how to solve problems as they arise. You'll also begin to notice how many foundational concepts repeat across Adobe products—layers, timelines, keyframes, effects, masks, and adjustment-based workflows—which makes learning new tools faster and more intuitive over time. Growth here comes through use: testing ideas, refining timing, revisiting concepts, and diving deeper only when the project calls for it.

Most importantly, remember that the software is here to support your vision. As the mechanics of using the tools fade into familiarity, what rises to the surface is taste, rhythm, and storytelling. Because these chapters are a starting point, you're encouraged to continue exploring from here—through online tutorials, templates, etc.—as part of an evolving practice. Let each project sharpen your instincts and expand what you know is possible! **Keep building. Keep exploring. Let's make cinema!**

NOW
F*CKING
GO

Thank you for coming along.

I wrote this book with you in mind.

My goal was simple: to share everything I know in a way that feels clear, accessible, and usable—without gatekeeping or unnecessary complexity. I wanted this to be the book I wish existed when I was finding my way into AI and AI-driven cinema and filmmaking. This technology is still so new, and what you're holding is truly everything I've learned so far. I'm still learning every day—and that's part of the excitement.

My love for AI art goes far beyond interest—it's obsession. From day one, my mind has been continuously blown by what's becoming possible. When I scroll through the Midjourney Explorer page, I don't just see images—I see entire films waiting to exist, every frame feeling like a story trying to unfold. What matters to me isn't what's trendy or dismissed as "AI slop," but creating work that means something—work that inspires and stays.

From the beginning, I approached this book with that same intention. The layout, pacing, structure, and visual rhythm were designed with care so the experience of reading feels grounded, calm, and focused—because clarity is what allows ideas to move forward. The design of the book isn't just for decoration—how I sectioned and boxed certain elements is part of the thinking. Everything I know, you now know. I didn't hold anything back. There is no hidden layer, no private club, no second book you need to unlock later.

I want to see your films. I want to be moved by the stories only you can tell. I want to be surprised by how your ideas unfold. I want to see you win awards. I want all of us to win. My grandmother used to say, "You didn't come this far just to stop now." That idea stayed with me and it's why I didn't want to leave you halfway through the process or drop you off without the full picture of how to actually finish and render your film.

If this book helped you feel more confident, more capable, or more motivated to create, then it has done what it was meant to do. *Thank you for coming along. I'm rooting for you.*

EXPLORE THE

DREAMING IN DIGITAL

COLLECTION

Dreaming in Digital
"The Age of AI Art"

Dreaming in Digital
"Interior Design and Architecture in AI Art"

Dreaming in Digital
"Fashion and Beauty in AI Art"

Dreaming in Digital
"The Age of AI Cinema"

About the Author

K.A. Betancourt (Kantrell Betancourt) is a creative director and visual storyteller working at the intersection of cinematic production and emerging technology. With nearly two decades of professional experience across editorial design, photography, and 2D and 3D visual production, her work reflects a long view of how creative tools evolve—and how artists adapt alongside them.

A ***Forbes***-recognized voice in AI and creative practice, Betancourt created the Dreaming in Digital guidebook series to help creators move beyond novelty and toward clarity, intention, and authorship. Rather than centering on tools or trends, her approach emphasizes cinematic thinking, visual judgment, and the discipline required to finish meaningful work. While software and platforms will continue to evolve, her focus remains on helping creators develop confidence, taste, and narrative clarity that can outlast any single tool.

She is the founder of Eight17 Studio, an AI-driven creative studio focused on cinematic storytelling and visual innovation. Through workshops, speaking engagements, and the Dreaming in Digital series, she continues to expand access to AI filmmaking and visual storytelling for creators at every level.

Tools & Disclosure

Programs used to create this book include the following:

Midjourney
Google (Nano Banana)
Higgsfield AI
Runway AI
Adobe Photoshop (AI Editor)
Adobe InDesign (Book Layout)
Adobe After Effects

OpenAI's ChatGPT was used for grammar refinement, organizational support, and general research assistance—including summarizing publicly available information, clarifying terminology, and supporting editorial structure. All creative decisions, interpretations, layouts, and conclusions remain the author's own.

Information about the programs referenced in this book was gathered from publicly available sources, including official documentation, company websites, and general reference materials.

All images in this book were generated using AI-based text-to-image systems. Visuals are derived from original prompts written by the author, as well as prompts developed collaboratively during the writing process. Any resemblance to existing AI-generated images or previously published works is purely coincidental and unintentional.

www.ingramcontent.com/pod-product-compliance
Ingram Content Group UK Ltd.
Pitfield, Milton Keynes, MK11 3LW, UK
UKHW060018051026
15591UKWH00003B/264
9798994516003